Insecurity

Ultimate Guide to Overcome Relationship Jealousy

(How to Overcome Social Anxiety, Relationship Jealousy)

Jonathan Donnelly

I0558280

Published By **Simon Dough**

Jonathan Donnelly

Insecurity: Ultimate Guide to Overcome Relationship Jealousy (How to Overcome Social Anxiety, Relationship Jealousy)

ISBN   978-1-998927-27-2

Legal & Disclaimer

Table Of Contents

Chapter 1: Understanding Insecurity

Understanding and accepting lack of self belief is the first step to finish freedom and happiness. Let's begin this adventure by using records this emotion this is draining all of the immoderate exceptional power for your lifestyles.

Insecurity is a totally complicated emotion. It can without issues be expert through the use of in fact each person however it's miles very tough to recognize. Emotional lack of confidence can cripple someone's potential to create good sized relationships. It is a direction to destruction. An insecure individual cannot definitely experience happiness and internal peace because of the truth the feelings of self-doubt and vulnerability are simply too sturdy. If you're emotionally insecure, you're in a very risky role. You are depriving yourself of the threat to stay a glad and big lifestyles.

Insecurity is more not unusual than you agree with you studied. Even individuals who seem proud and confident have their personal self-doubts. Surprisingly, even lovable ladies and effective men have insecurities too. Everyone has his or her private manner of dealing with this complicated emotional hassle. Some pass extraordinary lengths actually to hide their emotions of inadequacy. Insecurity thrives in severa regions of human beings's lives. It is in particular commonplace in relationships, specially if one of the partners experience weaker or smaller than the opposite. It is commonplace in the workplace too. Even a effective CEO can be eaten up via emotions of loneliness and self-doubt. Insecurity is a hurdle that you should triumph over if you need to acquire your entire capability.

We all cope with lack of self guarantee in a unmarried manner or some other. In certain instances, it can additionally be an top notch supply of strain and motivation. However, being too insecure can prevent you from reaching small obligations. How do you assume to acquire your desires even as you don't even don't forget in yourself? It will prevent you from cultivating healthful relationships with human beings around you. How do you count on to revel in your existence if you are constantly haunted with the aid of the sensation of inadequacy and vulnerability?

Don't allow lack of self belief control your lifestyles. With a aware try to combat your bad emotions, you will be capable of create a greater wonderful self-photograph that might help pave the road for actual happiness. Fighting lack of self assurance isn't an clean journey, but the advantages are actually sincerely worth it.

Once you overcome the feelings of lack of confidence and inadequacy, it is going to be less complex so that it will experience existence's easy joys. Once you've got were given a better view of your self, you may attain extra. A notable self-photo performs an vital component in accomplishing happiness.

If you have not any problems approximately your conceitedness you may with a piece of right fortune enjoy the small pleasures of life.

Dealing with lack of self assurance isn't always an smooth challenge. It is a protracted manner that consists of a deep knowledge of your non-public fears and dreams. If you want to conquer lack of confidence, you can must have a study your non-public weaknesses. Building self warranty starts offevolved with a self-control to try to beautify your very own self-photograph.

Insecurity may also need to make you enjoy vain, unimportant and powerless. At first, it'd seem no longer feasible to get out of the situation. However, as soon as you make a decision that you need to stay a higher lifestyles, you could begin looking for methods to put off your self-doubts and emotions of inclined point and vulnerability. This starts offevolved offevolved thru improving your very non-public self-image. You want to make a determination to have a laugh your flaws and to love yourself but your imperfections. Once you examine to triumph over yourself-doubts, you may slowly re-construct your out of place experience of self. This is best feasible if you could truly receive who you are without pretensions.

If you experience down and susceptible, the device may sound a piece an excessive amount of for you for now. Let me guarantee you that it's miles feasible to triumph over loss of confidence if you are decided and dedicated. Everything in this e-book might be meaningless in case you aren't determined to enhance your lifestyles. On the opportunity hand, the adventure can be easy if you dedicate yourself to converting your perspectives.

Keep in mind that there can be no confident method that facilitates people overcome loss of self belief. Each individual is special and every story is top notch. What may work for some other character may not be simply proper for you. What is probably easy for you might be tough for some extraordinary. Do now not compare your revel in with the studies of different human beings. This is your journey, and you need to not rush yourself or strain your self to revel in better. Take subjects as they come but decide to improving how you experience about your self.

The avenue to loving your self begins offevolved with expertise your present feelings and present scenario. You need to actually accept that you are insecure an awesome way to make a strength of will to alternate. It is high-quality to start via the use of comprehending the complexities of your very own lack of self perception. Acknowledge the sources of your personal emotion to sincerely apprehend in which your vulnerability is coming from. Digging into your poor feelings will offer you with an perception about your lousy self-photo. This could probable look like a tough step however is important on the way to surely achieve happiness.

You don't rush the gadget, and take time to get delight from each problem. Do now not strain your self each. You should be emotionally prepared for you if you want to efficiently discover ways to love your self yet again. It seems like a hard manner but ultimately, you may be capable of enjoy a excessive satisfactory of lifestyles.

This e-book will manual you via the steps of improving the way you feel about your self. If making a decision to have a look at the relaxation of this e-book, preserve in mind that there aren't any hints. This e-book will most effective assist you understand your emotions and way your feelings. This ebook includes quite a number of pointers to make you experience higher approximately your self, however the magic will quality paintings if you without a doubt preference to be happy. Open you're your coronary heart and get maintain of that your life may be higher.

Let's begin via locating the terms in your research of lack of confidence. I expect that lack of confidence manifests itself in loads of techniques however the fashionable feeling that it offers human beings can through the use of hook or by means of way of criminal be summed up. Based by myself studies and primarily based on what specific human beings are telling me, the following are the most common research and manifestations of loss of self belief: it's like a jail, it leaves humans with a feel of inadequacy, it turns people into perfectionists and it makes people compare the whole thing.

The Prison of Insecurity

Insecurity will make you feel like a prisoner. If you are insecure, you don't have the freedom to revel in your existence. Even excessive excellent feelings like happiness, exhilaration and pride are impossible to experience because of the fact insecurity is simply getting inside the way all the time. Insecurity will alienate you and preserve your coronary heart in a very dark area.

Naturally, you want to break out this prison of emotion. So possibly you got up one morning and decided that you want to be ok with yourself. You concept that you can convince yourself to be satisfied over again in a right away. That is really now not feasible. How are you able to expect to be happy in case your emotions are all snarled because of insecurities and vulnerability?

There is no instant treatment. You can't break out your very personal bad feelings in only eventually. To without a doubt experience pinnacle approximately your self, you have to untangle all of the lousy emotions you've got. Try to apprehend why you feel prone and awful. It looks like an prolonged method but every step is crucial of you in reality need break out.

Once you get away your insecurities, you will find out it less complicated to cultivate your relationships. You will discover it less complex to experience extraordinary emotions like happiness. You need a pleasing self photo in case you want to live a lifestyles of pride. Don't allow loss of self warranty to take over your life. Let's try to get away your jail by way of way of slowly trying to apprehend your feelings and feelings.

The Feelings of Inadequacy

Your lack of self assurance will regularly depart you feeling small and inadequate. If you're insecure, you are likely struggling with emotions of failure and unhappiness in severa areas of your existence. Insecure human beings often experience like they fall quick in areas of marriage, friendships and profession. The awful emotions are fueled by using the use of identifying your identity alongside aspect your achievements. In effect, whenever you're making errors, regardless of how huge or small it's miles, you experience inadequate and incapable.

The emotions of inadequacy can be overwhelming. It can be specially painful whilst you experience a flood of unexplainable terrible emotion with out an cheaper explanation. It can be prompted through a smooth mistake like lacking a lessen-off date or failing to make a sale. Perhaps you even beat yourself up for no unique cause in any respect. You may additionally simply find out yourself

You need to understand that matters will not get better if you are prettier, smarter, greater a achievement or thinner. You can not spend our entire existence wishing that things may also need to trade. No one is measuring you and your abilties. Learn to truely accept your flaws as a manner to be less tough on the manner to love yourself truely.

Also apprehend that human beings don't love you based totally on what you may do or what you cannot do. Relationships are not primarily based on achievements so don't worry approximately no longer being the extraordinary. It isn't possible to be top notch. It isn't always possible to recognize everything. It is impossible to pride everybody.

Use your flaws and mistakes to build your person. They are a massive part of who you're. Use the past to analyze. Use your inadequacies to be more compassionate. Loving your self method loving every single part of your self, now not truly the factors which you like. Don't make your "inadequacies" make you enjoy together with you worthless.

The Pursuit of Perfection

Being a perfectionist appears like a first rate detail doesn't it? After all, it honestly manner which you have a desire to eliminate flaws and defects. The pursuit of perfection surely appears like an superb quest, however don't be fooled. Being a perfectionist way that you are too scared to be inclined and willing

This preference of perfection and this desire to eliminate all flaws is surely a completely clear manifestation of lack of self belief. More often than now not, perfectionists try to collect perfection because of the truth they may be scared of judgment. They don't want to be seen as insufficient and inclined and so that they compensate with the resource of seeking to be exceptional all of the time.

Being a perfectionist is tiring or maybe lonely. You will typically grow to be feeling disenchanted with yourself because of the fact perfection cannot be finished. Don't be scared to fall a chunk quick or to be 2d area. Don't placed an excessive amount of value on the opinion of dad and mom which can be judging you.

The Grass is Not Greener on the Other Side

Do you usually think that the existence of numerous humans is better than yours? Are you jealous of numerous humans's seemingly greater snug manner of life? Do you sense such as you deserve greater than what you are becoming?

Wealth, beauty, manner of lifestyles, opportunities- do you experience like precise people have the whole lot higher than you do? You likely have a pretty extraordinary life however you've turn out to be harassed and sad. Don't waste some time specializing in what one in every of a type humans have. You will definitely feel depressing due to the fact you don't popularity on the essential matters in existence. Count your advantages. Learn the way to recognize life because it takes place.

It can also additionally appear to be amazing humans have higher topics going for them however you simply in no way understand what they will be going through to make that kind of judgment. You ought to probable see their massive houses or their version-thin our our our bodies and style designer luggage, but do you apprehend what's internal their hearts? You don't understand what superb humans are going thru so that you can't exactly say that their lives are less difficult or better.

You want to forestall evaluating your existence with the lives of different people due to the fact you are not in a contest. If you preserve on evaluating your lifestyles with the lives of various human beings, you received't be capable of truely understand all the superb subjects occurring in your existence. You received't be capable of recognize the benefits that come your way if you preserve on looking at the benefits of different humans. Keep in mind that exclusive humans's lives need to not be a yardstick of the way you have to live your life. Their fulfillment received't make your own achievement plenty less massive. People who're certainly happy have the potential to be happy for specific human beings.

Instead of measuring your achievements closer to the achievements of other people, attempt to locate your non-public niche. You can absolutely offer you along with your personal definition of fulfillment based mostly on what makes you happy.

If you are bored with feeling inadequate and nugatory, keep analyzing and we allow you to regain your vanity. Let's keep with the useful resource of seeking to pindown the purpose of your terrible emotions.

Chapter 2: Sources of Insecurity

Where is this sense of inadequacy coming from? It is vital to understand the muse reason of your lack of self warranty for you to start an prolonged-time period healing approach. Let's have a take a look at the sports of your life and try to discern out what's inflicting you to experience this inadequacy.

Insecurity is part of human nature. Even the maximum confident person you've ever met need to've felt insecure in a few unspecified time inside the future of his or her life. To a exceptional volume, it's miles a very healthful emotion. It method that the insecure man or woman recognizes his or her very personal weaknesses and boundaries. More importantly, an insecure character sees room for improvement.

Yes, it's miles certainly possible to look your very own vulnerable factor and enjoy amazing approximately it.

The technique is to apprehend it and receive it. If you revel in locate it irresistible's something that you could decorate on, then create a plan a good way to assist make subjects better. On the alternative hand, in case you experience like it's no longer some thing you could control or exchange then don't live on it. Don't make a huge deal out of it. None people are described via our shortcomings and weaknesses, so don't make a large deal out of a small mistake. Be humble sufficient to genuinely accept which you are not an outstanding man or woman.

Unfortunately, it's far hard to hold this form of thoughts-set.

It is straightforward to permit a small insecurity to eat you up. Before you realise it, a small lack of self notion can also need to turn out to be a large ball of feelings that you could now not control.

Your personal insecurities and bad feelings can be extra viable if you apprehend the reasons. You can best resolve the trouble sincerely if you dig deep into your very non-public emotions to try. No maintain in thoughts how difficult it seems, you should attempt to understand the roots of your feelings.

Trying to dig into the darkest factors of your coronary coronary heart may be a completely tough adventure, but you will best learn to love yourself in case you realise the reasons on your loss of confidence. This is the number one and maximum vital step. Once you find out your self inclined to open up your coronary heart, restoration and happiness will come in advance than you expect.

Do you recognize the reasons of your lack of self belief? We all have our motives for feeling insufficient, and our reasons is probably tough to recognize on occasion. To assist you apprehend your present day-day-day emotions, have a look at thru the ones not unusual reasons of loss of confidence, and try to figure out how yours started:

Feeling Unaccepted

In the perfect international, individuals who rely would love and take delivery of you for who you're, what you don't forget in and what you do. However, it's far sincerely not possible to satisfaction everyone. There are people who will decide you and criticize you. Sometimes, even if others imply properly, they though come to be making others experience unaccepted. This feeling of rejection, especially from cherished ones, may be a big reason of lack of self assurance.

You are very fortunate if you have a loving family who enables you in any way they may be able to. However, those who love you very an awful lot every so often revel in like they may be in the characteristic to criticize and decide your lifestyles. Because they hold a unique role for your life, they may enjoy like they may be entitled to observation approximately everything that they don't take delivery of as genuine with.

It can be tiring and heartbreaking to pay interest people you adore communicate negatively about you and your alternatives. Naturally you will enjoy rejected and unaccepted. You will experience like you are continuously being attacked even in your private home.

Rejection creates lack of confidence as it leads you to believe which you are not suitable enough. The more you attempt to please your circle of relatives, the more you could experience insecure whenever they reject your efforts.

No depend how lots you want your family, you shouldn't stay your lifestyles trying to please them.

If you found that the sensation of rejection at home and the sensation that you aren't time-honored thru your circle of relatives are the reasons of your loss of self notion, your first step to recovery is self-splendor. This technique that you must no longer are in search of the approval of various human beings inside the entirety which you do. It is good enough to pay attention to their evaluations but don't their criticisms ruin you. If you want and get hold of your self for who you're, you may be stronger in accepting what others say about you. You can be greater company approximately your selections despite the fact that others don't approve. You can be happy irrespective of the truth that outstanding human beings are saying horrible matters. If you are taking delivery of your self, then you can however be incredible despite the fact that great human beings don't get hold of you.

Loss and Tragedy

As a child, you probable had a favorite toy or pillow that gave you consolation every time you felt scared or by myself. You in all likelihood had a protection blanket that made you experience stable no matter what you possibly did or who you confronted. If you are like maximum adults, you have got were given possibly thrown away your teddy go through or your pillow thru now. But what you don't recognize is that even in case you already

22

grew old, you still have your protection blankets. They have truly superior into subjects which may be more grown-up and complex.

Perhaps you positioned out to find protection on your project, to your economic institution debts, for your houses or even in your own family. There is sure to be something or a person that offers you consolation. Now imagine losing that supply of safety.

Just like a little one who is getting to know to sleep with out a protection blanket, you'd probable enjoy very scared and virtually insecure.

Are you insecure due to the fact you recently went via the tragedy of dropping someone or something critical to you? Are you want a infant who these days out of area his or her safety blanket?

Loss is a totally painful enjoy. If you latterly misplaced a person or some thing essential to you, you may have massive hollow on your coronary heart. This sudden exchange may leave you empty and willing. Without your source of comfort, you'll in all likelihood experience by myself and insecure.

The prospect of going through the area without your safety blanket is horrifying. It will leave you inclined. It will depart you insecure. Did you latterly lose a few component this is very important to you? Did a completely unique person in your lifestyles depart you alone? The tragedy of loss includes the ache of managing how to circulate on. It is indeed hard to stand the sector without your supply of self assurance, however you can't live in the darkness all the time, are you able to?

You want to take into account that the power you want to face the sector is some aspect absolutely indoors you. You must take delivery of as real with which you don't need a few aspect or every body due to the fact you've got your self. Your most effective deliver of security ought to be your non-public inner energy and self warranty. Once you provide in for your weaknesses, it might get tough to look that you don't really need something or every person. You genuinely have to upward push about the pain of loss so as experience entire and stable.

Serious Life Failure

Do you experience like no longer something goes your manner even in case you pour all of your efforts into a few thing a brilliant way to make it paintings? It can be irritating to no longer discover satisfaction in any vicinity of your existence. If now not some thing seems to be going your way, then your spirits will really be overwhelmed. A series of tragedies may additionally want to suck away the self notion and happiness to your veins. When things get too anxious and disappointing, you could possibly experience insecure.

Sometimes, destiny may be virtually harsh and existence may be too tough. There can be times even as you experience at the side of you not have the energy to address all the hardships that lifestyles throws your manner. It can get frustrating. When topics don't turn out the way you planned, you can with out problem lose your self guarantee. It can simply be tiring to dream if no longer something you recommend ever comes actual.

Before we hold, you need to invite yourself, "Am I searching on the right course?"

Chances are, you're without a doubt searching on the awful aspect of your lifestyles. There are likely 1000 of specific topics happening to you however you are in reality too blinded via manner of your frustrations. You are without a doubt that specialize in the incorrect things so that you can't recognize the advantages that come your way. You are insecure because of your personal angle. You refuse to look that there may be some component lovely within the good deal.

Stop magnifying the terrible information and awareness at the topics that might make you smile. If you recognize wherein to look, you could considerably beautify your extremely good of life. If you focus at the super things, it's far going to be less complicated as a way to be stable and happy. I am now not announcing which you want to ignore the awful stuff. Those are very actual issues which you need to stand everyday. You simply need to re-orient your lenses to consciousness on the subjects which can make you happy instead of factors that make you sense pissed off and disappointed about your existence.

Poor Body Image

In this factor in time at the same time as paper-thin models grace mag covers and billboard commercials, it is able to get very difficult to be cushty in a unmarried's non-public pores and skin. How are you able to be cushty with your frame in case you understand that the norm is to be lovely and first rate?

Unfortunately, your body can be a supply of intense insecurity. I am sure which you may think about at least three subjects which you want to enhance about your bodily appearance. Do you watched that your waist is simply too large? Your face is simply too flat? Your frame constructed is simply no longer right? Your frame may be a great deliver of lack of self guarantee. The beauty and cosmetics employer are making billions truely because of the truth majority of the population of the planet is not satisfied with how they appearance.

It does no longer help that most fashions and celebrities frequently have digitally superior pictures. As a rational person, in all likelihood you apprehend that this general is in reality not applicable for regular people. However, for optimum teenage ladies who nonetheless have a completely fragile view of themselves, this sort of popular is a deliver of intense lack of confidence.

Women are specifically insecure about themselves. Very few women will possibly tell you that they may be satisfied with the way they look. It can be very tough to feel glad if you aren't glad with what you spot inside the replicate. It can sincerely get pretty tough to like yourself if you could't even do not forget incredible adjectives that you can use to provide an explanation for your self.

Take a tremendous look of yourself on the reflect. Are your frame components entire? Are your organs functioning properly? Are you able to do topics in conjunction with your body? If you are, then you definitely definately have many things to be pleased about. You are blessed with a body this is practical and specific. Don't waste it slow trying to meet the standards of various humans on the identical time as you recognize that you have already got what you need.

Learning to like your frame is an prolonged approach that starts offevolved offevolved with searching after your self in preferred. Perhaps you experience depressing due to the truth you received weight over the last few years. If you likely did, possibly it's time to attention for your health by way of using the usage of exercising and mastering how to plan a proper eating regimen. Maybe you don't like your hair, then possibly it's time to drop thru the salon for a higher reduce. Perhaps you aren't happy in conjunction with your pores and skin, perhaps it's time to strive beauty lotions so that you can deliver out your herbal splendor.

Taking care of yourself is not arrogance, never. Taking care if your body is the essential first step that could educate you to love what you have. Eventually, you'll recognize that society has evil standards that can without a doubt make human beings revel in terrible. If you need to virtually love your body, you want to start thru taking toddler steps.

The desired of splendor isn't the identical for everyone, every area and every way of existence. What may look hideous to you could look lovely for specific human beings. Try to peer what ought to is lovely about yourself and use that to assemble a pleasing relationship together with your body.

Remember, you best have one body. You would possibly in all likelihood as nicely learn how to locate it irresistible because of the reality it's miles the only one you'll have in this lifetime.

A Rough Past

Psychology has already showed how important someone's formative years is. It can form your persona, your beliefs and your frequently taking place mind-set in the direction of lifestyles in preferred. Some humans are blessed with a stunning teenagers entire of glad memories. Unfortunately, there are folks who look lower lower back on their early years with a heavy coronary coronary coronary heart.

You will recognize that you are a mature man or woman if you could get over what happened inside the past. You have become a real adult in case you apprehend that you can't spend your life dwelling on topics which may be already over. If you can get over all of the awful topics that occurred on your adolescents, then you definately definately are a actual person. We recognise that this isn't smooth. For a few, this might even be a totally sensitive problem. Nobody can modified what happened, however hold in thoughts that you may continuously exchange your thoughts-set. Don't appearance again with anger in your heart. Even if it's miles real which you had a horrible time in your more youthful years, deliver hobby to the prevailing to look how blessed you're. Look on the stunning possibilities of the destiny earlier of you. Look on the parents which are willing to love you and recognize what you do.

Your existence is a awesome deal too precious and you could truely enjoy an entire lot of stunning topics if you don't stay at the horrible. Your young people doesn't outline you. You have manage of your destiny. Don't waste your years in the world with the resource of living on some detail that you could no longer exchange.

Focus all your power on subjects that you may however manipulate. If you think about a horrible event that you can no longer trade, your view for the rest of your lifestyles is probably dark. How are you capable of understand the stunning matters taking area to you if all your electricity is focused on some component that you can not even exchange or manage?

You can't alternate your beyond however you may manage your present and your destiny. Why don't you interest on topics that make you happy or subjects that make you experience blessed? Surely, there are various matters that you could sit up for in case you want to popularity at the positives.

Psychologists may also moreover truly be proper in claiming that a person's early life has a large effect in his or her individual lifestyles, however recollect, you may constantly exchange. You can update your adolescence reminiscences with lovely studies which you encounter in your normal life.

Talking to people approximately your past will extensively assist you recover from the terrible opinions you may have had. Be open to searching out the recommendation of mother and father which are willing to be happy yet again.

This era is experiencing a modern-day form of insecurity brought about with the useful resource of the use of the internet and social media. In the following bankruptcy, we're able to investigate how technology gave this era a new form of lack of self warranty.

Chapter 3: Technology and Your Insecurity

It is an undeniable reality that generation is taking on our lives. Unfortunately, it isn't always in reality innocent. It may be a deliver of loss of self perception too. Read directly to discover extra.

There is not any doubt that generation drastically made our lives less tough. It made conversation quicker and it made groups run more successfully. However, on the quantity of human feelings, technology is inflicting us harm. Real-time actual communication is being changed by excellent chat programs and friendships are being modified thru various social media applications. Unfortunately, this form of environment is giving us a cutting-edge and precise way to experience insufficient. Yes, technology is inflicting this period to be even greater insecure than they already are.

In this day and age, most people non-public a smart cellular phone and a pill. We use it to maintain our relationships. If you don't have a social media community account, then don't forget yourself lucky. It is slowly proving to be certainly one of the most important reasons of loss of self warranty these days.

Stop Comparing

With social media, it is simpler to appearance how humans are dwelling their lives. It is straightforward to see your immoderate faculty mortal enemy turn into a warmth version. It is straightforward to look your boyfriend's ex who seems to be the image of a amazing partner. It is easy to look how everybody is getting married or having infants. With those styles of records for your hands, it's far difficult now not to gauge your own achievements in evaluation with the achievements of different humans.

When you be aware some of these colourful updates about special humans, you begin to consider how clean and notable their lives have to be. A photograph of a chum in Tokyo or a colleague along with his own family is all it takes that permits you to query your private happiness. All the reputation updates and exceptional pictures may probable make you sense insecure about your very own lifestyles.

When you keep in thoughts it, no considered one of their proper minds have to publicly put up personal and sensitive troubles on social media. You wouldn't see a socialite housewife located up about her circle of relatives's extended listing of money owed. You wouldn't see an artist publish about his struggles in making a mark. You wouldn't see a a achievement CEO publish approximately her dishonest husband.

With social media, it is simple to count on that different people have much less complicated lives. If you high-quality see the exceptional things, you aren't seeing the entire picture. Other humans don't have much less complex lives. You sincerely assume that they do due to social media.

So prevent stalking other humans on-line. Stop thinking about the lives of various human beings. Stop the use of on line social media networks if it simply makes you experience like your existence is insufficient and miserable.

Stop Creating an Online Life

Other human beings deal with their insecurities with the useful resource of growing an Internet existence that is virtually splendid from fact. They do that to make human beings consider that they're glad no matter the reality that they will be now not. Don't create an internet man or woman with the beneficial resource of posting high-quality fame messages or pix to wholesome your dream life. Don't placed up pictures of pricey matters if you recognize which you certainly can't avoid those gadgets. Try to make certain that your on-line lifestyles is in keeping with your real existence. Social media could probable strain you to be a person you are not however don't provide in. Make positive that what you challenge on-line is similar to how matters are in reality.

Don't get affirmation primarily based mostly on the amount of buddies you have got got or primarily based absolutely definitely on the type of feedback which you get thru posting your image. An on line buddy isn't always the same as a real buddy. In the give up, what topics extra is the happiness you definitely sense. Even if you do obtain making different human beings consider that you are glad, the whole thing can be vain in case you don't genuinely feel happy interior.

This lack of self belief because of era and social media is particular to parents which can be dwelling on this generation. Our grandparents did now not have the identical problem. For the extra conventional regions of lifestyles which can be often affected by a person's insecurity, take a look at right away to the following bankruptcy.

Chapter 4: Insecurity in Various Areas of your Life

Insecurity could have an effect on diverse components of our lives. Even if it is hidden deep inner us, it is able to still arise itself very strongly. Here are the unique regions of lifestyles that are generally laid low with lack of self assurance.

Life is continuously changing. What can be strong now may be rocky in a while. As we increase up, we discover ways to cope with whatever surprises that lifestyles can also moreover throw our manner. However, there are times whilst it honestly gets too hard to cope with problems. Often, there are areas of someone's life which feels truely inclined. These are the areas that are rocky and inclined. These are the areas that could make a person insecure.

Since you can not limit your insecurity outstanding on one precise region of your life, you in all likelihood have overlapping reports of loss of confidence. You may additionally

additionally experience insecure about your economic reputation in recent times and then feel inclined approximately your marriage day after today.

Insecurity normally assaults the maximum inclined areas of a person's existence. Here are a few additives which make people insecure.

In romantic relationships or marriage

At one factor for your courting, have you ever ever ever ever felt which you are genuinely not outstanding sufficient? Insecurity in a dating, specifically in marriage, can be very lonely. If you have were given lack of confidence troubles, you in all likelihood see issues in regions wherein none surely exist. You blame your self for small subjects that reason you to anxiety and argument. Do you placed you're the usage of your associate away because you are so insecure? It's time to restore up and make your relationship higher.

No, now not restoration up the connection.... Fix up yourself.

Yes, the best manner you can flip this round is with the resource of getting to know self-popularity. You can enhance your courting by the use of beginning to love yourself. You can most effective be a higher associate in case you apprehend that you need to be cherished. You can accumulate self-love in plenty of techniques. Try to attend to your frame more. Engage in sports activities sports sports activities or find out a hobby. Don't make your marriage the tremendous deliver of your emotional success. Nourish your other relationships as your marriage grows.

Keep in mind that arguments are ordinary. No vast courting is surely clean always. An important a part of being in a splendid dating is understanding a way to manage subjects collectively. Don't blame your self if topics bypass incorrect. The point of being in a relationship is taking element in a journey collectively. If being in a relationship is without a doubt making you insecure and paranoid, then maybe you aren't organized for this lovely journey truely however.

In Social and Economic Status

When you notice the wealth of people around you grow increasingly, it can be hard now not to feel insecure. This is mainly real whilst you're operating tough to collect your desires however not anything you do seems to make matters better. Financial protection is specifically critical for providers and breadwinners. To a sure quantity, coins is important because it will allow you to acquire your simple wishes. However, don't make coins the deliver of your safety.

If you enjoy like you're very inclined due to your economic recognition, you could work on instructing your self that allows you to make wiser monetary state of affairs. Make a plan of strategies your destiny is going to look like. Make a smart funding portfolio so you obtained't have to worry about your retirement.

Do what you could to boom your financial savings and investments- however do the whole thing with the information that money can disappear.

Work tough and try to make smart investments, however understand that there aren't any ensures. If you are making money the supply of your protection, you're in a very willing area.

In Your Professional Life

Perhaps you recommended yourself which you'd be in a certain powerful feature via way of now. Maybe you made a incorrect profession preference inside the past. Maybe you left out a totally precise enterprise employer possibility. Point is, if you haven't executed your profession desires but, you are probable willing too. After all, most folks need to make a mark within the international. Those who have now not located their motive however must revel in insecure and lonely.

Again you want to consider that your interest does not define you. A CEO of a multinational enterprise isn't always extra vital honestly because of the reality he has a immoderate characteristic in an workplace. Of route, it is vital to find out a efficient profession as a manner to keep you busy. Having a technique is likewise vital in case you want to have sufficient coins to offer to your family. However, hold in mind that your profession does not define you. Do now not allow it to be the anchor of your safety.

In your circle of relatives existence

A family is meant to be amongst your primary sources of power. However, there are times even as relationships even alongside facet your very private blood-partner and kids don't work out properly. It isn't unusual to see households getting torn apart for diverse motives- on occasion, the reasons are even unimportant and meaningless. If your circle of relatives is falling aside, you would absolutely sense insecure. Such a history can also need

45

to have an effect on the alternative important regions of your life. You in all likelihood received't be able to broaden a wholesome courting with other humans because of trust troubles.

Having hassle collectively with your own family will clearly depart you inclined. After all your family is the corporation of folks who should truly get keep of you and love you. They must be supportive and loving.

We all understand that own family relationships aren't usually happy. You really should boom up and gather something state of affairs you're confronted with. Don't use your own family insecurities to ruin the rest of your relationships. Try to apprehend that if some thing goes wrong along with your own family, you are in all likelihood not the great character responsible.

Chapter 5: Look into Yourself

If you really want to heal, you don't ought to appearance some place else. Start with your self...begin together together together with your coronary coronary heart. You need a exchange of angle that allows you to see that a person consisting of you deserves love. You deserve love from others and you deserve love from yourself.

As you go through the numerous troubles of lifestyles, you could observe that one of the most vital topics that you may examine is to maintain shifting ahead. You need to rebuild and adjust your angle irrespective of how tough a scenario appears. Overcoming lack of self assurance method having the capability to look happiness wherever you pass. This is the reward of not giving into disappointment and melancholy. This is the reward of ultimately learning to simply accept your very own flaws.

Are you equipped to start the adventure of analyzing the way to like your self? If you're, then start studying on. After studying your insecurities, we are now prepared to definitely heal by way of using manner of driving away all of the negative feelings delivered approximately via loss of confidence and vulnerability.

Change Your Self-photo

Insecurity starts offevolved if you have a very horrible perception of your self. For example, in case you experience inclusive of you can not benefit a venture or if you assume which you are inferior in contrast to others, you are basing your evaluation from a horrible self-photograph. Whenever you enjoy like you're placing your self down, prevent yourself from filling your thoughts with bad mind. Think of satisfied thoughts that allows you to highlight your strengths as a person.

I understand that it may be hard to save you yourself from having a poor self-photograph while you've already spent years and years on your very personal prison of lack of self notion. However, you can not allow your insecurities control you and your existence anymore. Recognize and take delivery of your insecurities so that you will get over these terrible emotions. Control your mind so that you will now not provide into typically feeling terrible about your self.

It can be a very tough enjoy to struggle it out collectively collectively with your very very own demons however it's miles pa art work of growing up. You can exceptional certainly be a mature adult if you may take shipping of your flaws completely. The temptation to truely stay in mattress to have your very personal pity party will constantly be sturdy. Whenever you are tempted to in fact stay in mattress, maintain in thoughts which you want to fight your very own weaknesses if you need to enhance.

The undertaking is intellectual, emotional and mental. You will only win in case you don't supply in on your very very very own awful thoughts.

Changing yourself-photo consists of a deeper statistics of yourself. Consistently spend time meditating about your existence and your ideals. Write down unique mind in a magazine in case you assume that they'll assist you growth a extra excessive wonderful mind-set approximately subjects in fashionable. Think approximately your strengths and blessings. Learning to like yourself is all about seeing the great matters in you. It is all about doing what makes you revel in specific, and cultivating relationships that assist you turn out to be a better character.

As you are taking infant steps in the route of the very critical purpose of a contemporary self-image, surround your self with right things and correct humans that make you experience appropriate. You want all styles of encouragement within the early components of this process. It pays to have someone with whom you may communicate to each time you are feeling down. Open up to a pal or a relative whom you determined may be able to apprehend your very non-public worries. If you are in a wedding, take time to speak to your big one of a type and allow her or him comprehend that you are attempting hard to beautify your self for the relationship. Let your partner realise that you want her or him to be part of this journey.

Take this time to beautify your relationship with your self. Stop all of the self-hate and the self-bashing. Stop making your self experience unhappy with the useful resource of usually thinking that you can't gain what you need. Be your very very very own cheerleader. Be your private number one supporter. Your existence may be lots simpler in case you are at peace with yourself.

An important part of this adventure is spotting and accepting your very personal flaws. You can not be actually happy if you don't understand the terrible factors of your existence as nicely. You need to maintain in mind that having the ones flaws is ok. More importantly, you want to keep reminding your self that you love and you are loved irrespective of a variety of those flaws. You aren't much less of a person actually because you cannot strength. You will now not be loved greater if you are thinner. You are not insufficient honestly because you probably did not get your university degree.

In extraordinary phrases, don't try to determine you fee via making a list of what makes you a "marketable" person. Know that ultimately, what subjects is your capability to love your self definitely no matter all the terrible topics which might be keeping you down. Know that you can rise above.

This very first step of the adventure is critical and crucial. Once you keep near this step, the opportunity steps can be a top notch deal much less difficult.

Change Your View approximately the World

Once you've got got a greater remarkable view approximately your self, this could be a bargain easier. Think of the arena as a playground, now not a place. You are not in competition with extraordinary humans. In the give up, the most essential topics in life isn't about the way you obtain fulfillment or how plenty coins you are making. It's all about the manner you assemble relationships and what kind of love you're able to supply and attain.

Do not compete with different humans. Do not see the arena as some thing you need to triumph over. Always face up to the temptation to revel in advanced. You do now not want to triumph over anybody else. You do now not need to be greater beautiful. You do no longer want to be greater a success. In the prevent, the ones aren't without a doubt the topics so as to make you a happier person.

Try to offer you along with your very personal definition of achievement. Find your area of interest and preserve on with doing matters which you expect leads you to find out your feature in existence. Not everybody are intended to be wealthy felony professionals of successful business organisation. Not everybody is meant to be a scientific medical health practitioner or a pilot. It's k to be regular. If you find out delight and happiness in staying at domestic collectively together with your kids, then you definitely virtually are more a achievement than an insecure version who struggles to be traditional inside the style global.

You will meet individuals who will make you word the beauty within the topics spherical you. Stay with the ones people. We all want the affection and aid we can get from special human beings. Allow others to help you make the process less complex and smoother.

Let me emphasize time and again that existence isn't a opposition. Don't make everything a competition at the identical time as we're all without a doubt struggling to discover our personal kind of happiness. Look for folks who can cheer for you. Look for humans you need to cheer for. You don't want terrible feelings and terrible human beings in your existence at this factor.

Take the manner as some component grade by grade. You can exceptional honestly exchange your attitude of the area while you've changed your thoughts-set of your self. Don't try and do that collectively. It is probably too hard to really attempt to benefit the entirety all at one. Use all of your focus and electricity on developing one detail and flow into on as you accept as true with you studied you've succeeded.

Build Strong Relationships

Tear down that wall you've got spherical your self. You probably constructed that as a safety mechanism for all the lack of confidence and awful feelings that you feel. Work on making robust relationships with those who be counted wide variety to you. Repair some element that you discover crucial and massive. Life can be plenty extra huge if you have unique people by manner of your trouble.

Is your marriage on the rocks due to your very private insecurities? Try working on that first. Work on making your accomplice experience higher about what you have got were given, Make her or him revel in specific and cherished. Stop seeking out guarantee and reality, and really revel in your lives together. Stop questioning that you could manage the course of your relationship due to the reality you can't. For now, all that you could do is sit down decrease back, live collectively and try the entirety to make your relationship ultimate an entire life.

Do you've got good sized friendships? Try to create and domesticate together with your pals. You can be capable of find emotional achievement when you have friendships that don't harbor competition and lack of self belief. Don't move for buddies that push you to having bad thoughts approximately your self Don't have buddies who just want to compete with you. Try to create genuine relationships that deliver out the remarkable in you.

Are you patching matters up together along with your own family? It can be tough to have a healthy relationship together with your family inside the event that they remind you of criticisms and a horrible common mind-set. However, you want to be mature approximately taking in what they're pronouncing. I can assure you that if you have a notable self-picture. It could be less complicated a good way to take in something they're pronouncing. You is probably able to snort at their complaint and shaggy canine story approximately vital matters which used to have an effect on you lots. No depend what people say, having a healthful relationship at the aspect of your circle of relatives will extensively make you experience better about yourself.

When I will let you realize to beautify the relationships to your existence, I am not telling you to make every unmarried one in each of your enemies your pal too. Some topics are actually no longer viable to build up. You don't really need to truly receive all and sundry on your lifestyles. Learn to clean out people. You can be civil with extraordinary human beings but you don't need to absolutely accept them. Be clever about growing your relationships. The humans spherical you can considerably have an effect on what you think about your self. Be realistic in deciding on.

Learn to Love

I am not speaking about romantic love. I'm speaking about learning a way to take care of different human beings through small but honest acts of kindness. I'm talking about understanding the way to understand and knowing the way to be compassionate. I'm studying about a way to offer and a way to gather. I'm talking about expertise the way to make matters better through smooth gestures that show exceptional people how accurate the arena can be. Yes, I am speaking about the large L-word, love.

The international could be a far greater lovely region if we comprehend the way to do small subjects with massive love. Our relationships may be greater significant if we don't compete with one another. Small acts of kindness might also moreover want to really help decorate topics. Your functionality to present a chunk greater may even exchange a few other individual's life.

This is not an clean undertaking, I understand. In truth, it is able to be fantastically difficult to start this addiction if you aren't used to it. However, with small steps, you can get used to it. Wouldn't it is gratifying to recognize which you are spreading the love thru your small acts and sort phrases?

Surprising as it may sound, the ones acts of goodness and love allows you recover from your insecurity too. Knowing that you spread kindness will make you enjoy higher approximately yourself. Thus, loving yourself and developing a incredible self-photo is made lots much less tough.

Learn to Accept Love

One of the quality indicators that you are becoming over your lack of self warranty is analyzing the way to take delivery of love from particular people. This is in reality extra difficult than it sounds. Learning the manner to really accept love technique that you genuinely expect you're suitable enough to deserve love from the people spherical you.

If you have a terrible self-photograph, it could be difficult to assume that one-of-a-kind humans can love you completely. After all, you in all likelihood assume that there is not something to love about you. Only on the identical time as you see your right rate will it's far clean if you need to certainly accept the love that special people are willing to offer you. Only a first-rate self-picture will make you understand that there definitely you need to be cherished no matter your wealth or achievements.

Accepting love can be hard at instances even as you enjoy unlovable. Accepting love can be tough on the identical time as you're continuously unhappy or angry. You acquired't receive as proper with that one-of-a-kind people can love you if you don't see the beauty on your lifestyles and on your character. To be able to simply receive love, you have to first have a outstanding self-photo.

It can pay to recognize that normally, love isn't always conditional. People who surely love you could now not give up on you irrespective of what form of character you've become. They are inclined that will help you if matters get too difficult. However, if you are insecure, you may probably locate it not possible to consider this. You will simply tire out exceptional humans through the usage of no longer accepting the love that they are willing to offer you.

Be Happy for Yourself and for Other People

In the cease of the whole lot, you'll be able to experience proper delight and peace whilst you get out of the prisons of your loss of self perception. This is not a short way. In truth, it would take years and years. However, while you overcome your personal insecurities, it will probable be simpler as a way to be satisfied for yourself and to be glad for distinct people.

If you are insecure, you cannot be truely glad because you are generally fearful of dropping the instantaneous. You want to be happy all of the time so you need to manipulate the emotion and you panic of the idea of losing in. You may also definitely sense euphoric but this kind of happiness is fleeting. The kind of happiness that stable humans experience is calm and peaceful. They might not enjoy happy all the time however they will be good enough with it. It is not loud however it's miles right. Secure people enjoy a peace a thoughts due to the fact they don't try to manage their happiness.

If you're strong, it'll likely be a lot much less hard to revel in happier for different humans too. You received't need to continuously be in competition together collectively together with your friends. You percent their delight if something exact takes location to them. You don't get jealous in case you aren't in an further accurate characteristic. You truly experience satisfied due to the fact they may be pleased with what they finished. Keep in mind that secure humans apprehend that unique people have one of a kind resources of joy. They don't compete with one more. They don't attempt to reap what different humans have finished surely due to the fact they assume that there's best one direction to happiness. Secure human beings understand that the happiness of a mom can be one-of-a-kind from the happiness of a infant. The happiness of your buddy can be top notch out of your happiness.

In the prevent, stable people have the self guarantee to locate the direction to their very non-public happiness. They are inclined to walk precise roads to find out what is going to definitely cause them to satisfied and fulfilled. Don't get me wrong, they get really bad days too. However, they address awful days with a pleasant attitude and a perception that things gets better.

Do you located which you already located your happiness? Read the subsequent bankruptcy in case you want to live satisfied, confident and solid.

Chapter 6: Staying Happy

It lets in to increase conduct at the manner to hold you satisfied and strong. Here are a couple of behavior to help you live satisfied even in some unspecified time in the future of your toughest instances.

Life's twists and turns may wonder you or maybe if you already placed your happiness and safety, you may lose it in an instant because of an unexpected problem or tragedy. It lets in to start behavior in an effort to keep you brilliant. These conduct are apparently small and simple but they will can help you get thru even in the course of the hardest instances. If you want to live regular and happy, begin those behavior, and you may with out problems get thru whatever existence may additionally moreover throw your way.

Keep a Philosophy of Gratitude

Always be pleased approximately the blessings that are available your lifestyles in diverse paperwork. Be thankful for even the high-quality matters that make you smile. Even there are a load of terrible problems that is probably thrown your way, try to find out the silver lining in every state of affairs. No remember how terrible topics is probably, you have to normally discover some thing to be pleased about.

If you experience fat, be grateful that you have a wholesome frame. If you sense terrible, be grateful that you have meals to devour. If you enjoy unpleasant, be grateful which you have garments to position on each single day.

If you train your eyes and your thoughts to think this manner, it will be simpler so as to see subjects beyond any form of issues or hardships. Remember to take a look at the big photograph and maintain in thoughts that you have what it takes to get via any warfare that comes your manner.

It is right to begin writing subjects which you are thankful for on the prevent of every day. Keep a mag on the way to remind you of the first rate topics in existence. No recall how terrible your day is, write some thing to your mag. During your darkest hours, test through the pages you've written. It will extensively assist you bear in thoughts that subjects will get better.

Talk to Yourself

Always spend time trying to find your middle. Don't get over excited by way of the usage of way of the topics which is probably taking vicinity in your existence. If you don't spend time reflecting to your modern state of affairs and thoughts-set, it is straightforward to lose attention.

Be self-conscious. Knowing in which you are, how you're dealing with matters and what you need to do will substantially assist you stay happy. It is lots a good deal much less complicated to be insecure if you experience like your life is a complete mess. If you're self-aware, you understand your emotions more and more. The more you apprehend your emotions, the extra difficult it's miles in case you want to experience awful about anything you are going thru.

Cheer for your self in something scenario you locate yourself in. You want to be your non-public cheerleader. Don't allow lousy days to get you down. Talking to yourself will assist you do not forget which you have a purpose to be glad regardless of some trouble you are going through.

Being self-conscious is a form of damage manipulate. It will save you you from growing damaging thoughts in an effort to deliver lower once more insecure mind. Knowing in which you are and the way you revel in will put together you for anything terrible feelings or conditions you could encounter within the future.

Surround your self with Positive People

The people you spend time with are very influential. If you surround yourself with shiny and sunny individuals who make you experience correct approximately yourself, it is much less tough to miss about some thing terrible mind you have in thoughts. If you're with folks that could make you revel in accurate about your self, you may have no time to suppose that you are inadequate and inclined. If you surround your self with fine people, you've got had been given a beneficial resource system which could deliver you well electricity to face some thing troubles will come your manner. Wouldn't it revel in higher to loaf around with those who genuinely do not forget in what you may do and in what you could obtain?

It does no longer mean that you will be glad all the time. It virtually technique that you can draw power and manual from each other at times whilst lifestyles gets too tough. Being glad and amazing does now not constantly suggest that someone has a grin on his or her face. You also can draw resource from folks who see that perfect in you.

This does now not recommend that there may be no vicinity for negative humans for your life. If you've got have been given the electricity to welcome them for your life, then pass in advance. However, hold in thoughts which you need satisfactory human beings in the end of times on the identical time as matters get too tough.

You can be a amazing man or woman for one-of-a-kind those who want you too. The understanding that you could offer strength and proposal to others is a good supply of motivation and strength to live targeted. Why need to you resist any opportunity or state of affairs which could assist you to convey moderate to the existence of various human beings?

Try to boom actual friendships with first rate humans so that you can truly advantage emotional fulfillment from your friendships. Learn the manner to accumulate out and to speak in confidence to folks that are continuously to your element. Friendships can be much less hard to maintain in case you aid one another particularly in the course of times of want and problem.

Don't Overanalyze Everything

Overanalyzing a high quality situation or trouble can also reason undesirable thoughts. If you've got got got too much time for your palms, you will probable simply grow to be evaluating your existence with the lifestyles of some other person. You would probable study why his or her lifestyles is higher than yours. You'll have terrible mind because of the reality you're evaluating your achievements. You may also moreover again and again examine the behavior of your companion. This would possibly reason seeing problems that are not for your courting in the first area. Stop trying to interpret his or her terms and motion. If you accept as true with you studied something is probably wrong in your courting, communicate to him or her without delay so that you can get a right away solution.

Also, attempt to prevent overanalyzing what other human beings might imagine about you.

Most human beings become insecure after they recall what are in different people's concept. Chances are, you may really grow to be with terrible mind on the way to make you experience willing and insecure.

The top notch way to prevent overanalyzing matters is to have interaction in huge hobbies that provide you with personal achievement. If you don't have an entire lot of time in your palms, you received't have time for idle mind.

Chapter 7: Identify the Source of Your Insecurities

"Our problems are man-made, therefore they may be solved by the use of man. And man may be as big as he desires. No problem of human destiny is past human beings." – John F. Kennedy

The first step to conquer any trouble in life is to pick out out its reason. You need to trace matters backward that allows you to understand a manner to drift ahead. This technique furthermore applies to defeating one's insecurities. Before trying to conquer a few element, you want to begin with knowing the source.

This step is critical because of the truth it is from this step that each one elements of motion shall take vicinity. Once you have got recognized the supply of your insecurities, you understand whole properly what you are up in competition to. If you are notwithstanding the fact that burdened, some of the not unusual sources of loss of self warranty are: being surrounded thru manner of over-achievers, being underappreciated, being omitted and rejected, being added approximately thru necessities of society and having low self-esteem.

When you are surrounded via humans who've their achievements putting on their chests, there may be a dishonest that permits you to experience a sure pang of jealousy towards them. Don't worry; this is regular. However, the manner you act on this jealousy makes all of the difference. Some humans deal with this jealousy as a motivation to work more hard so one can benefit the identical sort of success. On the alternative hand, there are individuals who address this jealousy as a deliver of devastation because they revel in like they can in no manner gain the identical form of success. Insecurity develops at the same time as you're continuously surrounded with the useful resource of these styles of humans. When absolutely everyone round you is doing nicely on their very private, humans will be predisposed to evaluate you with them.

Comparison regularly continuously leads someone to expect what may be wrong with them, and it makes someone ask questions collectively with what do different people have that he/she does no longer have.

If you are continuously inside the agency of over-achievers and you are not doing some detail about it, some humans may also moreover underappreciate your capabilities and abilities and might address you as if you have been invisible, but this is not a motive as a manner to be discouraged; most importantly, you should no longer think lowly of your self genuinely due to the fact distinct humans do that. If there are those who've to experience lowly of themselves, it's far the ones those who deliver you down. Don't allow what different people can help you apprehend dictate the manner you live your existence. As you may see afterward, the talents of these "overachievers" are not the best abilties within the global, and these should now not be the great requirements for appreciating someone.

Moreover, rejection isn't the forestall of the location. Just due to the reality other humans depart you out does no longer advise that you have to permit yourself to be neglected. Insecurity is often evolved in folks which can be continuously neglected due to the fact they'll take transport of the feeling that they will be not desired and that they cannot contribute a few factor extraordinary. As a way of combating in opposition for your insecurities, you may use rejection as a way of improving your self with a view to avoid this sort of feeling inside the destiny. Do now not use it as a depressant! Show the ones human beings that they made a mistake in leaving you out.

One of the largest motives of lack of self perception is while one is surrounded via societal norms/standards. The society wherein we belong to often has a perception of what is considered "right," "stunning," "handsome," and so forth. However, they fail to renowned that these necessities are tremendously bendy and can be bended at any time. Still, many human beings do no longer apprehend about this pliability and the end result is feeling awful approximately themselves when they do now not conform to those necessities.

Lastly, low vanity branches from a mixture of the abovementioned commonplace reasons of lack of self belief. When you do no longer have self-self notion and also you do no longer take shipping of as true with in your self, then you could continuously experience insecure about each little element.

Now that we have supplied some of the maximum common causes of lack of confidence, it's time so that you can come to be aware of yours. Identify yours now in case you need to preserve to solving your troubles!

Acknowledge Your Fears

"Don't be terrified of your fears. They're not there to scare you. They're there to let you understand that something is virtually worth it." – C. Joybell C.

After you have were given identified the supply of your insecurities, then you also are at the manner of identifying your fears. It is incredibly feasible that the deliver of your insecurities moreover includes the supply of your fears. For you to find out, you have to be goal and a keen observer.

What precisely are you afraid of? Take time to assume—list all the topics that you are feeling insecure of, and listing all the subjects that you are terrified of and the way they make contributions for your lack of confidence. Common examples are disappointment, rejection and no longer being proper sufficient within the eyes of others. Acknowledge the ones fears; for on the identical time as you renowned them, it manner that it is clean to you what precisely they are, how they've an effect to your lifestyles, and it makes you undergo in thoughts what you want to do approximately them.

For example, you worry sadness and rejection. Disappointment may additionally moreover are available precise bureaucracy— disappointment out of your dad and mom, out of your friends or maybe from your self. But why ought to you worry unhappiness? It is flawlessly ordinary. People make errors all the time; absolutely everyone is capable of disappointment. When you fear unhappiness, you're taking time to test your each motion to the thing that you are already appearing like a robot: very scripted and slightly transferring out of unfastened will. Does this result in remarkable results in your life? No.

When you worry no longer being actual enough in the eyes of others, then you definitely are permitting your insecurities to take over your life. Who cares what specific people say? As we shall speak later on, societal norms are created with the aid of manner of people too. These norms are not normally right. They do provide a few form of order in this chaotic global, however while people become too engrossed in them, the ones norms emerge as a source of issues due to the reality human beings already allow themselves to be managed via manner of them.

Face your fears. The only way to fight the enemy is to apprehend the enemy.

Chapter 8: Consider Your Strengths

"Nothing can dim the mild which shines from within." – Maya Angelou

As come to be mentioned in advance than, humans have a propensity to expand insecurities after they anticipate they're not proper sufficient and they don't have the crucial abilities to be ok with themselves. This have to now not be the case. Every character has his/her very private particular strengths, but every so often we take matters with no consideration, which includes our strengths. However, nobody-of-a-type character can pick out your strengths extra efficiently than your self. The most that exclusive humans can do for you is to manual you in the way of understanding what your strengths are, but the confirmation need to come from you.

How do you pick out out your robust areas? There are hundreds of strategies to do it, however one way is to endure in mind the matters which make you enjoy the happiest and maximum fulfilled. What is that trouble and/or hobby which you need to do all the time? What is that component which you are constantly craving for? What is that detail that offers you a sense of contentment and self-success? What are the subjects that you can do with out problem? Try answering the ones questions, and you'll be able to select out your sturdy areas quickly sufficient.

Take sports activities sports for instance. Some human beings are taken into consideration appropriate in sports, and they admit that sports activities sports are their strong vicinity because of the truth they experience gambling sports activities sports, they discover sports sports a very relaxing and captivating hobby, sports activities excite them and they may play sports sports sports activities without an awful lot trouble. Try the use of those standards in different regions that allows you to discover your sturdy regions.

Do no longer be afraid to remember your strengths. Stop telling your self that you are not right enough. You might not be professional in a certain vicinity wherein a lot of people excel, but there's usually an area which you have awesome abilties on. If you're notwithstanding the fact that unaware of what your strengths are, it will be useful to discover a number of possibilities in case you want to discover what the ones are. If you're already privy to your strengths but you in reality discover it difficult to renowned them, it's time that allows you to prevent this line of wondering.

If you sincerely preference to build up your arrogance and defeat your insecurities, you need to begin with considering your strengths.

Acknowledge Your Successes and Achievements

"Success is peace of mind it truely is a right away give up end result of self-satisfaction in understanding you in all likelihood did your remarkable to become the great you are able to becoming."– John Wooden

If ever you experience like you've got were given never completed something for your lifestyles, you are incorrect. Surely, there ought to be a few issue which you have completed in the beyond which you need to be glad with. Instead of living on your "failures" and inside the times at the same time as you felt which you aren't enough, why don't you try dwelling for your a achievement instances? Try to recall what those successes are and make those your using forces to conquer your insecurities.

These successes can are to be had one-of-a-type office work. If you agree with you studied that the achievements you word in specific people are the exceptional achievements there are on this global, then you definately are incorrect. You actually have finished some thing on your existence; you are not paying much hobby to it due to the reality you're degrading such achievements. Remember that every fulfillment is something to be proud of, regardless of how huge or small they'll be. Do no longer take them as a proper.

What may additionally need to those achievements be? Educational achievements are common ones. Extracurricular achievements are every other. But achievements suggest greater than trophies on one's fingers and medals around one's neck. You can say that you have additionally done a few component when you have helped others grow to be higher humans—for instance, a person goes through a virtually tough degree in his/her existence, and also you had been able to deliver him/her low-cost advice that helped him/her afterwards. Another instance is: you may say which you have completed some issue if you have successfully uplifted someone's spirits. Let's say that your buddy is having a horrible day, however you stored him/her corporation, and on the quit of the day, he/she advised you that he/she is thankful which you have been there and that you furnished a supply of consolation. These also are achievements,

85

pleasant intangible ones. But no matter the reality that those are in reality little matters, those are also things to be satisfied with; those display which you are not a useless character. You have well truely really worth on this international, and you have to understand with the resource of now which you have to continually see your properly really worth notwithstanding the truth that unique human beings do not due to the fact there'll constantly be individuals who can say which you have finished something profitable in your existence.

Acknowledging your successes and achievements is likewise a useful way of discovering your strengths. If you have got finished numerous subjects in a selected place, then there's a large opportunity that this place is your sturdy point.

Ask Friends to Help You Identify Your Best Qualities

"Encourage, improve and make stronger each other. For the first-rate electricity unfold to at the least one can be felt through us all. For we're associated, each one." – Deborah Day

It has been stated earlier than that only you can pick out out what precisely are your strengths—but your friends can also assist you with it. Ask folks who are closest to you to help you choose out out your wonderful characteristics. Choose the set of friends whom might be sincerely sincere with you. Ask them to jot down down down down or to inform you the tendencies about you that they determine upon maximum.

Once you have got have been given gathered a listing of your great skills from the humans you're taking shipping of as actual with the maximum, hold this listing with you and use it as a source of motivation. When matters go wrong, certainly skip again to this listing. When you sense such as you've been a completely terrible character, take a look at this listing, and you will see that you aren't one. You will see that particular humans can see you for who you really are, and no longer truly as a made from the requirements of society. The exquisite that you may do is to remember in what your buddies indexed down—due to the fact those are the functions that they see as an observer. You can constantly deny which you private these trends, however take into account that actions speak louder than terms. You can also deny which you are not this form of man or woman, however your pals can attest to it that they see you as one with those adorable abilities.

Furthermore, it's far beneficial to do this exercise due to the fact 1) it's going to help you come to be privy to your strengths better; 2) it's going to assist improve your self-esteem due to the fact you may be reminded of the topics that people like about you; and 3) you can have the chance to enhance the competencies which aren't mentioned as your "superb" ones.

Looking at this listing of developments, you can check out whether or no longer or no longer these are your robust characteristics or now not. It will help increase your self-esteem because it will remind you which you aren't worthless. And most significantly, you could see from an observer's aspect of view the property you are proper at, and you may be able to take it from there the areas or the tendencies that you are not that correct at. This should no longer be a supply of lack of self belief however as an opportunity as a motivating pressure for development.

You already have the policies of a steady individual with the aid of manner of using first-rate characteristic of those tendencies, and you can continuously add extra features on your "nice" list via striving to beautify your self.

Chapter 9: Surround Yourself with Supportive People

"Every man or woman goals help from others so as to reach his/her dreamland." – Euginia Herlihy

One of the excellent methods to triumph over lack of self warranty is to be surrounded through folks who guide you within the entirety you do due to the reality insecurities are only made worse in case you pick to surround yourself with people who deliver you down.

Surround your self with people who are not judgmental, folks that are willing that will help you accomplish your purpose of overcoming your insecurities. These human beings can be your circle of relatives, your buddies, your big unique and most specially the ones folks that are present system the same kind of healing way. The final business enterprise of human beings is the best guide corporation that one may also moreover have because of the reality in this u . S ., you're surrounded via the those who recognize exactly what you are going through, and collectively, you can come up with solutions in your issues.

But this doesn't endorse that your family, pals and/or associate do no longer don't forget as large. They are also very essential resources of suggestion and power because the road closer to converting yourself and your perspectives isn't an smooth one. There will usually be instances at the equal time as you will revel in like giving up because of the fact changing one's thoughts-set can't be executed in an right away—it calls for severa hard artwork, but having a resource organization thru the use of your facet can constantly ease the burden of your issues.

Another large motive why a guide group is vital is that those people understand you for who you're; they might likely be the identical those who helped you give you your "awesome qualities" list. Thus, that those humans can be honest to you no matter what.

When a few component's incorrect, they may no longer hesitate to inform; on the identical time as matters bypass proper, they'll uplift your spirit. It is essential to be surrounded through technique of those forms of human beings because truthfulness to oneself and to others performs a totally vital characteristic in overcoming your insecurities.

Never underestimate the strength of a help business agency. They are always there for you, they may now not determine you and they'll be there to manual you alongside the manner.

Avoid Being Around People Who Make You Feel Insecure

"There are many proper seeds in you. Therefore you need to avoid each lousy soil within the global." – Israelmore Ayivor

In relation to the previous tip, it is critical to surround yourself with folks who make you revel in true approximately yourself and no longer folks who accentuate your insecurities.

Even if the said humans are the ones you've been spherical with for the longest time, in the event that they purpose you extra bad emotions than the nice ones, then it's time to permit them to bypass. Distance yourself from those people. When we have been surrounded thru the usage of the identical shape of humans our complete lives and we've visible them achieve one element after some different, it is able to produce the feeling of being left inside the once more of and being incapable of accomplishing something.

The simplest manner to forestall those insecurities from forming is to do away with the supply. Maybe the purpose why you can't save you feeling horrible approximately your self is due to the fact you are continuously surrounded by way of manner of the those who push yourself perception degree down, make you feel unappreciated, reject you and demand on the requirements imposed with the aid of society.

Why torture yourself? Why do you need to be surrounded through those humans? You don't. Beyond charming others, past conforming to society's requirements, you have to remember yourself first. Save your self from the emotional ache.

How are you capable of keep away from the ones human beings? Simple. Just strive. If you're used to being with those humans for your normal workplace, then it's time on the manner to get to recognize different people. Look for reasons to avoid them—those want no longer be lies, but there are loads of motives available. Engross yourself to your duties so that you don't ought to be aware about them. Sooner or later, you could see which you have efficaciously damaged unfastened from their enterprise and that their critiques now not take into account to you.

If they are the reasons for the development of your insecurities, then it's miles actually proper with a purpose to detach your self from them an amazing way to supply your self room to increase.

Socialize More

"Be certainly interested by each person you meet and clearly all and sundry you meet may be sincerely interested in you." – Rasheed Ogunlaru

It can't be denied that we generally have a tendency to overthink whilst we are by myself due to the fact there can be not anything to preoccupy our minds from wandering off to different sorts of mind. If you have already got lack of confidence troubles, then it's far notably in all likelihood that you'll regularly assume of these issues whilst you are by myself. When you spend too much time residing for your insecurities, they constructing up due to the fact you throw in a unmarried principle after every different. As a way to this trouble, you want to socialise with others extra, and attempt meeting new buddies that lets in you to prevent having an excessive amount of by myself time with yourself.

Meeting any character for the first time often makes human beings apprehensive. However, meeting new friends can certainly be an brilliant issue. New pals may want to make you find out your hidden strengths and competencies because precise human beings supply out one in all a kind elements oldsters each time we get to realise them, relying on your preferred topics of discussion. As the trade of thoughts goes on and on, you may see that your mind is now not focused in your insecurities but as an opportunity on the brand new subjects that you have found out out of your friends.

You have to undergo in mind how essential it's far to have pals to assist you while you feel down. Opening your self to top notch humans, socializing with them and constructing nurturing relationships will let you realize that you're no longer an lousy individual in the long run, contrary to what you first perceived yourself to be.

If you're not a completely sociable man or woman, that's no longer a problem the least bit. You certainly must strive. When pals ask you out, be a part of them. Who is privy to? Maybe you'll meet your satisfactory pal on that day. Some human beings are sincerely shy and are hesitant to socialise with others, however once you meet people whom you get at the side of, you could apprehend which you shouldn't have been shy the least bit, and you will wish that you've acknowledged those humans longer. In quick, do not be afraid to meet new humans. New people deliver unique surprises to our lives.

Lastly, don't forget that many buddies are better than few in phrases of imparting ethical assist to your toughest battles.

Identify What Hinders You from Overcoming Your Insecurities

"The brilliant way to address boundaries is to use them as stepping-stones. Laugh at them, tread on them, and allow them to guide you to a few element higher." – Enid Blyton

There are instances even as we are greater than willing to do something, however then some element is stopping us from executing our plans. The query is, what's this "some element," and how can you eliminate it?

This applies additionally to overcoming your insecurities. Let us anticipate which you are already clear approximately what your insecurities are, what you are terrified of and which you are inclined to defeat the ones insecurities; however then some thing is stopping you. Ask your self: what is blocking off your manner?

It is hard to attain this when you have barriers alongside your way, most specially if you have all the electricity of will and motivation, however a few factor else does no longer need you to hold. Still, preserve in thoughts that no journey comes with out boundaries. A journey without limitations often does now not encompass training for us to cherish. Identify what the ones obstacles are and make a waft inside the direction of having rid of these in order as a manner to begin defeating your insecurities.

Even even though there are barriers to your selected goals, do now not be discouraged. Remember that the ones obstacles are brief, and they may be referred to as "limitations" due to the reality they may be speculated to be surpassed. Establish that strength of thoughts to defeat your insecurities and maintain this stated energy of will in surpassing the limitations along your way, and virtually, no longer a few component can stop you from dwelling a lifestyles complete of success.

Another way to inspire your self is to assume of those barriers as benefits in cover. They can also block your manner and make your adventure difficult, however they'll certainly make your adventure properly worth it. They may be the supply of complications, unhappiness and doubt, but the give up-made from surpassing those obstacles is continuously a nice element to purpose for.

Do now not be discouraged. Will yourself to triumph over those barriers, and you could find out your self one step in addition in overcoming your insecurities.

Chapter 10: Always Make a Reality Check

"Reality is that which, while you save you believing in it, would now not depart." – Philip K. Dick

Sometimes, insecurities are evolved because of our paranoia approximately the matters taking area spherical us. Since this is the supply of the hassle, then the solution is to have a look at the artwork of putting apart imagination from fact.

This sort of loss of confidence typically takes place in relationships. When you are in a relationship with someone and also you experience insecure, you usually assume that you are not proper enough for your associate and/or your accomplice can also discover a person else because of the fact you do now not satisfy his/her requirements. Oftentimes, those forms of insecurities root from rumors and/or paranoia.

In this form of situation, the terrific problem so you can do is to get your statistics immediately first earlier than reacting to some thing. When one does not trust in himself/herself, he/she has a tough time debunking rumors and believing truths. This need to no longer be the case. Be as aim as you may and try to recognize the situation from an unbiased detail of view.

Consider this case: people in a relationship regularly fight due to the fact the girl often assumes that the character is as plenty as a few thing due to the fact "she will be able to see it in his movements," together with choosing up the telephone overdue; but she does not have concrete proof. She is insecure about their courting, so she claims that she will "see it falling apart," however what's wrong in this picture? She does no longer have any proof to decrease back up her declare. All of her accusations are rooted from her interpretations of the person's actions. What's with deciding on up the cellphone past due? Does this automatically propose that the relationship is falling aside? No. But this type of wondering will purpose a strained dating if it is persisted.

In this shape of scenario, the individual has did no longer make a reality check due to the reality she is simply too caught up along with her imaginary scenarios. The exceptional way to transport spherical this hassle is to prevent trying to have a look at minds. Stop looking for to placed meaning in every motion with out proper basis, for this may best cloud your judgment and could cause traces to your relationship with special humans.

Moreover, do not allow your insecurities to cloud your judgment. Do now not permit your insecurities take fact some distance from you; do now not permit insecurities make you lose reference to the fact.

Stop Comparing Yourself to Others

"Comparison is the lack of lifestyles of pride." – Mark Twain

One of the most not unusual property of loss of self belief is evaluation to others. There are hundreds of instances at the same time as this will not be avoided, most mainly if there are stark, apparent versions between you and the opposite individual. Although there are times whilst this is unavoidable, you want to even though do your quality to keep away from doing such.

Comparison to others often takes location at the same time as you notice things and/or inclinations in every one of a kind character which you do not see in your self. But the query to ask is how certain are you that you do not own the ones developments as properly? This is one of the risks of contrast— it prohibits you from figuring out your whole functionality due to the fact you're already putting in boundaries to your self as the opposite of a few different character.

Comparison furthermore takes location even as every other person has splendid abilties which you do not, particularly whilst those skills are your "annoyed" abilties. Another question to ask is how first-rate are you that you are incapable of these abilties? What if you only assume you are incapable of excelling in these sure areas, however surely, you have got the ability to be skilled in this place?

Comparison moreover brings risks at the same time as they will be carried out with distinct people. You cannot control what terrific humans will say approximately you; the fine trouble you may manage is how you may react to the ones opinions. Do not thoughts the comparisons that they make— you apprehend what you are able to, and also you comprehend what your feasible abilities are. Do no longer be blinded through the comparisons that they make; they're pleasant searching at you from a 2d-man or woman issue of view. It is you, the person, who subjects. Remember that genuinely anyone is specific.

Do Not Make Your Insecurities Obvious

"Don't permit worry or loss of self assurance prevent you from attempting new matters. Believe in yourself. Do what you adore. And most importantly, be type to others, even in case you do now not like them." — Stacy London

It is a given reality that you are feeling insecure about sure matters, but this doesn't suggest that you want to permit it show. Doing so can also best provide you with an photo of vulnerability. Show human beings that you are not affected, for a few issue they may say about you may add for your burden of defeating your insecurities.

Do not allow other people see which you are inclined. Project yourself as a sturdy person, even at the same time as you're though on the factor that you're trying to defeat your insecurities. Doing so could likely not pleasant help you via stopping unique people from perceiving you as inclined, however doing so may additionally educate you to turn out to be confident spherical distinct humans.

In relation to the tip to prevent analyzing minds, you should not count on that different humans can see that you have insecurities. Knowing, or truely questioning, that special human beings can see your prone element will best make you greater conscious and will make your movements extra confined. If you do the other trouble, however, nobody will need to have a take a look at the issues that you're going via.

Showing your insecurities to exquisite humans may most effective make them worsen; it is higher in case you hold them to your self and display best to the people whom you endure in thoughts.

Discuss Your Feelings

"If you've got got the words, there's always a chance that you could find out the way." – Seamus Heaney

Another fundamental way to triumph over your insecurities is to permit it all out. Discuss your feelings with a person else, particularly your top notch pal or someone who you apprehend will recognize you honestly. Letting all of it out is a way of acknowledging it, and whilst you renowned it, you understand what you're preventing in opposition to.

There is something very comforting about being capable of particular your emotions in truth. Keeping the ones types of emotions and emotions locked up internal you is difficult and reasons you lots of pain and anxiety. On the opportunity hand, letting those be recognized through the people you be given as proper with offers you a feel of safety and comfort. Remember that the ones humans whom you don't forget will not judge you for the way you experience, however instead they're there to make you experience higher.

Discussing your feelings with exclusive human beings isn't handiest beneficial to you as you may be given recommendation through distinct people, but it is also beneficial to others because of the fact they'll check from your evaluations.

If you discover it hard to speak approximately your emotions with precise people, do yourself a preference thru manner of at the least searching out a medium that allows you to specific your feelings. Do you often discover yourself misplaced in phrases of the spoken word? Maybe you'll express your self better in terms of the written phrase. Try running a blog or maintaining a magazine in which you could file your mind. This way, you don't need to permit the tension constructing up inner you. Moreover, retaining a report of your mind is also critical in terms of monitoring down your development of healing. At first it may appear like all your mag entries are entire of doubt and insecurities, but as you go on, you could see the changing style to your entries, and by way of the usage of then, you may see which you are making improvement closer to overcoming your insecurities.

Discussing your emotions does no longer first-class make the load a touch lighter, however it furthermore allows you to acquire advice from unique humans.

Remember That You Create Your Own Destiny

"The nice person you're destined to end up is the individual you make a decision to be." — Ralph Waldo Emerson

Similar to the concept which you want to no longer take a look at your self with others, consider that you create your personal destiny. Remember which you are a very specific man or woman and that you may continuously be capable to do subjects so long as you may it.

Do no longer be suffering from what awesome humans say about you. It is our picks, not special humans's, that determine what occurs in our lives and how we are capable of stay our lives.

Keeping in thoughts that you create your private destiny will assist you disregard some issue degrading or underestimating statements humans say. In addition to that, retaining in mind that you are on pinnacle of things of your private lifestyles is a terrific begin within the direction of defeating your insecurities. You must apprehend which you are the only who makes a selection what is outstanding for you, and you are the best who is aware about exactly what you need and what you're afraid of.

Live your lifestyles the manner you want to stay it, no longer steady with what society dictates. Yes, there are high-quality hints that want to be observed, but in terms of abilties and individual development, you must not be constrained to the labels society offers humans. As such, one of the number one reasons why you sense insecure is due to the fact you are not on pinnacle of factors of your private lifestyles, and also you allow unique people's evaluations to persuade you absolutely.

Instead of conforming to the entirety that society says, harm away if you want to. Do your very very own hassle. Do now not be afraid; you is probably even starting a modern-day style. You are loose to perform a little element you need as long as it is jail. In phrases of your improvement, lead your existence on this form of manner that you will gather happiness and self-success ultimately.

Remember that there may be no different man or woman who want to run your life however you.

Chapter 11: Take Risks to Change Your Behavior

"If you dare not some thing, then at the same time as the day is over, no longer whatever is all you could have obtained." – Neil Gaiman

No rely how tough it's far to face your fears, keep in mind that it's going to all be actually properly worth it ultimately. Take risks to trade your conduct in case you really desire to actually defeat your insecurities. There may be plenty of traumatic situations within the manner, however you need to acquire as proper with that you are capable of overcoming those challenges.

For you to be greater happy to take risks, strive weighing the short-time period and lengthy-time period results of your moves. As a rational being, via your evaluation, you apprehend in case you need to deliver the maximum extremely good results, and you already know with the intention to produce the outcomes an awesome way to advantage you higher and longer.

On the only hand, thinking short-term might fine lead you to suppose that risking hundreds of factors for the sake of defeating your insecurities is a waste of time. Because overcoming one's insecurities is a tiresome undertaking, it takes masses of braveness and danger to be successful. Some people suppose that they should no longer trouble addressing their insecurities due to the fact they are already "satisfied" and they're "already dwelling the life that they want," but is this the existence that they need to live for the relaxation in their lives? Will this brief-time period wondering benefit them? Only considering the immediate effects will not obtain the fine blessings.

Going to the other issue of the coin, taking into consideration the prolonged-time period consequences of your preference to defeat your insecurities will make you realize that there are quite a few sacrifices, alternatives and tough alternatives to be made. However, consider it: dwelling together together with your insecurities may be great in recent times, however will it however be pleasant tomorrow? If you observed lengthy-term, you will see that all the chance might be well certainly well worth it given the effective results of overcoming your insecurities—along side self-fulfillment, person and talents development, and so on.

Just due to the truth a project is hard does no longer endorse that it isn't always properly worth task. Sometimes, it's far in the ones tough duties in which we examine the best lifestyles instructions; and it's far in those responsibilities in which we now not splendid enhance ourselves as fast as we have got attained the quit reason, however we enhance ourselves even during the manner of doing those responsibilities itself.

There is not anything wrong with taking dangers despite the reality that the prevent stays unsure. Keep in mind that the training and the studies alongside the way are ones that you may maintain all of the time.

Develop Courage inner Yourself

"Courage is the most crucial of all the virtues due to the reality with out courage, you cannot workout every different distinctive feature continuously." – Maya Angelou

Alongside taking risks, you have to develop enough braveness to perform that. The struggle in the route of defeating your insecurities isn't an clean one, this is why you want to be robust in the way.

Following Maya Angelou's quote, you can't retain with out courage. You cannot retain to doing any of the hints supplied on this e-book if you do now not have the courage and the strength of mind to reap this.

A way of developing courage inside your self is to weigh the experts and cons of what you are about to do. As you may see, defeating insecurities has more pros than cons, for they personal prolonged-term effects, and accomplishing this purpose will exchange your existence forever. This ought to be enough to inspire a person to move for it.

Sometimes, the satisfactory matters in life are not purported to be completed without trouble. They need to be received through tough artwork. This is wherein courage is to be had in. Develop braveness inner your self, and you'll reach whatever you desire.

Consider the Negative Consequences of Insecurity

"Try giving up all the mind that make you revel in terrible, or perhaps truly some of them, and be aware how doing that adjustments your existence. You do no longer need horrible mind. All they've ever given you was a fake self that suffers. They are all lies." – Gina Lake

One of your greatest motivations to subsequently begin defeating loss of confidence is to keep in mind the horrific consequences that it entails. How is loss of self belief affecting your life? Surely it isn't always affecting your life in an tremendous way. Wouldn't you want to exchange some thing that does not have an impact in your life in a high-quality way? A list of the bad effects of lack of self assurance need to serve as a guide.

If that some aspect is not bringing about amazing outcomes on your existence, wouldn't you want to do away with this element? This is precisely the same for loss of confidence. You must recognize that lack of self perception does no longer do you any accurate. In fact, it reasons the exact opposite—you experience lousy approximately yourself, you do now not trust, your private growth is stinted, you can not maximize your potentials, and also you experience afraid to strive new subjects. Seeing that those are the terrible consequences of lack of self notion, isn't it enough of a warning call to you that you want to alternate?

A way to remind your self of those horrible consequences is to anticipate yourself in the worst situations viable. As you receive as real with your self, bear in thoughts it; ought to you need to stay your existence this manner? Would you be glad residing in worry, constantly unsure and in no way high-quality of some thing? These are truely pattern, imagined situations that you may consider; there are hundreds of others, but that is most effective a manner of illustrating how critical it's miles to weigh within the excessive quality and terrible effects of one's moves.

Remember that loss of self belief will now not do you any true, as a result you ought to paintings within the route of getting rid of this negativity to your existence. Not doing so also can lead the ones worst imagined situations come to be a fact.

Think of the Positive Effects of Overcoming Insecurity

"A pleasant thoughts-set might not treatment all your problems, but its impact will make it properly well really worth the try." – Jeffrey Fry

In relation to listing down the terrible consequences of lack of confidence on your existence, it is also crucial to weigh in the excessive nice outcomes. If the lousy outcomes can function your motivating stress to defeat lack of confidence, then the same is going with the splendid effects. In the method of trying to conquer loss of confidence, it will get very hard, however you need to preserve on. When you're doubtful or while you revel in including you can't move on in addition, actually consider the rewards expecting you at the stop of the complete approach. The entire device is a tough one, but you want to be confident that it's miles going to be simply nicely well worth it.

What are the possible brilliant outcomes of overcoming insecurity? Heightened vanity, better socialization with others, man or woman and private improvement are the numerous many effective outcomes of overcoming insecurities.

You should constantly maintain your consciousness at the high-quality facet of things and now not at the awful. Do now not reside too much on the horrible, for they will be purported to bring you down. Focus on the outstanding and permit this positivity to be contemplated on your persona, and you may see the difference that it makes.

Focusing at the excellent does now not first-class embody thinking about the fantastic consequences of your actions, it furthermore manner commonly looking at the acute aspect of things. When confronted with a difficult scenario, what do you do? A pessimist will surely give up and think that his efforts have gone to waste whilst an optimist will see this difficult state of affairs as an opportunity for private improvement and honestly as every other venture this is quite feasible to overcome.

It is constantly higher to stay at the top notch aspect of things as opposed to the horrible. Staying incredible amidst the whole lot will rate you no harm on the same time as being horrible will absolutely deliver you similarly down.

Think of those exceptional results, and accept as authentic with how excellent your life might be whilst you begin to revel in those outcomes, and in fact you'll be extra stimulated to fight in opposition to loss of confidence.

Always Be True

" When we turn spherical & come head to head with our destiny, we find out that terms (spoken) are not sufficient. I understand such a lot of people who are extraordinary audio gadget however are quite incapable of working towards what they preach. It's one detail to give an reason for a scenario & pretty a few special to revel in it. I realised a long term in the beyond that a warrior attempting to find his dream should take his concept from what he definitely does & now not from what he imagines himself doing." – Paulo Coelho

Yes, you are trying to exchange yourself. And nice, you want to cast off your insecurities. Despite those noble intentions, you have to recollect that it's far critical to live actual to yourself always. In the way of attempting to overcome our enjoy of worthlessness and/or loss of conceitedness, we usually tend to try converting our personalities into some other persona that is very considered one of a kind from who we clearly are. We emerge as being pretentious, trying to find to stay a life this is some distance from fact, one which we recognise will make specific people regard us quite.

There is not any nicely in this form of exercise. It is a given fact that you are walking your way within the route of overcoming your insecurities. That's an first-rate start. But it have to be achieved in an honest way. If you are trying to trade your self, then you certainly need to alternate yourself into a person this is basically who you're, now not a person whose individual has been brought about with the useful resource of societal norms.

What makes us faux? Societal norms. It can not be emphasized similarly that one of the reasons why people end up insecure is due to the truth once in a while they revel in like they do not agree to the "norms" or necessities of beauty, intelligence, and many others. What humans neglect is that those norms are most effective created by means of human beings and that the ones do now not dictate what is surely right and what's certainly incorrect, within the equal way that those norms do now not supply us an entire photograph of what's clearly beautiful or now not. For those reasons, we should now not fear going toward the ones norms.

We have to ruin loose from the chains of these norms for us to live an sincere and appealing life.

 Learn to Let Go of the Things That Make You Insecure

"You will discover that it's miles essential to let things circulate; truly for the cause that they're heavy. So permit them to move, permit pass of them. I tie no weights to my ankles." – C. Joybell C.

We were speaking about casting off the motive of the trouble for pretty a while, but this aspect needs to be emphasized over and over so as it is not forgotten. In order to transport on at the side of your life, loss of self perception-loose, you want to learn how to let move of the topics that provide you with those insecurities. There is a opportunity that these gadgets are very luxurious to you, specifically if those are parents which can be unique to you however make you enjoy lousy, however in reality consider the impact that they have got on you.

Nothing is right for you if it prevents you from displaying your loose will. You might probable count on for now that these gadgets are proper for you and they make you happy— but you want to take into account whether or now not or not these gadgets are inflicting you proper happiness or whether or not they may be really thriving off your inferiority.

It is first-rate to allow skip of the topics that harm you as opposed to to permit them to reason greater damage and cause irrevocable damage. Moreover, it is excellent to let flow into at an early degree so you will now not be too related to it the moment you decide that it isn't always appropriate for you.

Chapter 12: Accept the Things That You Cannot Change

"Understanding is the first step to elegance, and incredible with recognition can there be recuperation" – J. K. Rowling

As an entire lot as you preference to change your self, there are nevertheless topics that you cannot do, and also you need to recognize this if you want to simply acquire it. Accept the fact that you are able to making mistakes and that you can not remedy the whole lot, however the excellent that you can do is to decrease the damage introduced on your existence.

There are masses of factors in our lives that we cannot alternate, however it doesn't advocate we ought to now not perform a little thing approximately it. These subjects can be everlasting, but how we react to these items supply us a totally exquisite story.

As prolonged as you exert your extraordinary try to change, then that want to be sufficient. Since there are subjects that we cannot trade, the super component that we are capable of do is to embody these gadgets absolutely. See these items not as limitations, but be for the purpose that those are important components of lifestyles and that the ones are possibilities for growth.

Learn to in truth be given the subjects which you can't change so that you may not stay on them for too lengthy. Instead, act toward folks that you could exchange, and exchange this stuff for 1) the betterment of your self and a pair of) the betterment of others.

Maintain a Healthy Lifestyle

"Eat healthily, sleep well, breathe deeply, circulate harmoniously." – Jean-Pierre Barral

People think that lack of self assurance is a intellectual and intellectual problem and that it does no longer comprise the bodily body. The truth is, it does include the physical frame. In anything we do, we want to not overlook the significance of the bodily body due to the truth with out it, we cannot characteristic honestly.

Inasmuch as loss of self notion is a highbrow problem, the country of the bodily frame plays a completely important factor. An bad manner of existence is one of the elements why one feels insecure—while you are physically unstable, there can be moreover a bent with a purpose to be psychologically, mentally, and emotionally volatile. A healthful frame effects in a healthful mind, and a wholesome thoughts produces smart and rational selections based totally on fact and cause and in reality no longer on one's feelings.

Moreover, maintaining a wholesome manner of life contributes to higher energy of thoughts, particularly in phrases of our emotions. We cannot disagree that an bad life-style outcomes in imbalanced bodily strategies which have an impact at the way we characteristic.

Being healthy is not without a doubt being bodily healthful or emotionally wholesome. Being healthy is a combination of every factors.

 Work on Eliminating Your Insecurities One at a Time

"In order to transport forward, you can have to stumble alongside the way, but each falter to your stride without a doubt makes your subsequent step even stronger." – Lindsay Chamberlin

Nothing well worth having ever comes smooth, and one can not accumulate fulfillment in a hard task with most effective a unmarried step. Remember that a huge step is a aggregate of small, single steps, and that applies the identical for disposing of your insecurities.

It is apparent which you already have your goal set and that you are greater than inclined to collect this reason, however you need to don't forget that you can not try this the smooth way.

Instead of looking for to cast off your insecurities all on the equal time, attempt strolling on every of them one after the other, and you could see that you may be more green on the end of the day. Moreover, it's far better so one can paintings on preventing each loss of self guarantee one after the opposite as it will come up with more attention, and it will now not confuse you with the opportunity insecurities, most especially if the ones insecurities belong to first rate elements of human life.

There can be a loss of shortcuts in the approach of defeating your insecurities, but the prolonged route is regularly paved with life training and top notch studies.

Develop Your Skills to Boost Your Self-Esteem

"Every man has a selected skills, whether it's far positioned or now not, that more effects and naturally consists of him than it might to some different, and his very very own need to be sought and polished. He excels extremely good in his location of interest—originality loses its authenticity in a single's efforts to collect originality." – Criss Jami

Insecurity frequently consequences from the questioning that you lack any capabilities in besides and which you are incapable of getting to know any form of potential. This is not actual. Every man or woman has taken into consideration certainly one of a kind abilities; it genuinely so takes vicinity that there are common competencies amongst human beings, and people are caused think that those are the simplest competencies possible for one to gain.

You have to not be restrained via this line of questioning. There are countless possibilities with reference to ability improvement. One way of overcoming your insecurities is building up your vanity, and one manner of building your arrogance is growing your capabilities; for this reason, following this specific judgment, one way of overcoming your insecurities is thru growing your abilities. When you be conscious that you additionally have abilities, and that you are capable of these, then you may receive as real with in your self extra, and you may surrender to suppose that exceptional people are better than you.

In order to benefit this, you have to be inclined to strive loads of latest subjects. We have heard of the time period "hidden abilties," and that is real. There are times at the identical time as our capabilities are "hiding" from us first-class due to the reality we have now not explored sufficient possibilities for them to seem. Sometimes, abilities hide within the most weird of opportunities, but you need to not permit this weirdness prevent you from exploring the ones said opportunities. Who knows? Maybe your interests and abilities lie in the ones possibilities, and that the best reason why you haven't obtained those competencies is

133

due to the reality you have got got been so afraid in the beyond.

As hundreds as all people is precise, absolutely everyone is also precise and gifted. We are typically supposed to excel in a single or extra subjects, and you are not an exception. You can do it!

Start Taking Action

"Live your reality. Express your love. Share your enthusiasm. Take movement within the direction of your desires. Walk your communicate. Dance and sing to your tune. Embrace your benefits. Make in recent times truely worth remembering." – Steve Maraboli

This is the ultimate tip with the intention to receive in this ebook: take motion. Every tip on this e-book is probably deemed vain if you do no longer at least attempt to look at them in actual-life. For you to enjoy the blessings of being lack of confidence-loose, then you definitely definately honestly need to start with the preference to fight inside the path of it.

The hints supplied in this ebook require hundreds of self-control—strong strength of mind in truth. Succeeding in your undertaking of defeating your insecurities is an prolonged way, considering we are handling thoughts, emotions and personal dispositions. Still, recollect that not some thing is not feasible if you are truely as a good buy because the task. Do no longer be afraid to start taking movement. To emphasize similarly, there isn't always some thing incorrect in taking risks.

It all begins offevolved with a single step. Take that risk and notice the distinction.

How to Apply Key Ideas for the Best Results?

After providing 25 tips on a way to defeat your insecurities, this financial ruin shall provide a precis of every tip at the element of a few additional guidelines:

Identify the supply of your insecurities

Every time you revel in that lack of self assurance setting, seize a pen and paper and make a listing. This manner, you can resultseasily find out the topics that make you insecure, and you will without issues recognise what boundaries you are supposed to conquer.

Acknowledge your fears

You can in no manner conquer any fear with out acknowledging it first. Admit to your self what you're terrified of, after which paintings your manner in the direction of conquering these fears.

Consider your strengths

You do now not want to be immodest that lets in you to enjoy consistent, however it allows to understand your strengths so that you will no longer revel in underestimated thru other people. Think of that super detail in that you experience the warmest, and be aware whether or now not this region is surely your uniqueness.

Acknowledge your successes and achievements

When you got something, whether or not or no longer massive or small, renowned it. There want to be no success left unrecognized, for you want to do not forget which you worked hard to gain this stuff, some element they will be, and you want to be diagnosed for that.

Ask buddies that will help you perceive your extraordinary traits

It is first-class you who can grow to be aware about the proper people whom you agree with. You recognize who you are honest with, and the individuals who aren't afraid to inform you matters straight to the face. Explain your situation to those human beings and allow them that will help you.

Surround your self with supportive people

You are aware about those who must make you experience unique about your self and people who do the complete opposite.

Choose to surround your self with individuals who belong to the previous beauty, and you will see a massive alternate of issue of view in your lifestyles.

Avoid being round folks who make you experience insecure

If you definitely want to lessen off all of the assets of your lack of self belief, then you definately want to also choose to avoid being round folks who bring about those insecurities. It can be tough at the start, but keep in mind that it is higher to reduce them off early in preference to to allow them to make you experience worse. Socialize more

In order to enhance your self notion around specific people, be sociable. Do not be afraid to make buddies; do now not count on that no individual will including you as their friend. There will typically be people who might be interested in what you have to mention. Every individual has a special story, and you may in no way apprehend how plenty someone can change your life until you permit them in yours.

Identify what hinders you from overcoming your insecurities

Similar to identifying the sources of your insecurities, you need to moreover pick out what are the restrictions that prevent you from defeating those insecurities. What is stopping you? What is obtainable that is stopping you from creating a circulate? What is preventing you from converting yourself? Ask your self those questions first, and through the usage of answering the ones questions, you could come up with answers.

Always make a fact take a look at

Paranoia gets you nowhere. Before you select to accept as proper with in something, make certain that there are information to decrease back it up. There will commonly be human beings and mind who will attempt to bring you down, but you need to not allow them to achieve success.

Stop comparing your self to others

There is not any need to evaluate yourself to others due to the truth you're a completely precise person. You have your private strengths and skills, and you want now not take a look at whether or no longer you have got have been given the equal skills that others private.

Do no longer make your insecurities apparent

Learn to cover your insecurities so that you may additionally moreover keep away from being perceived as susceptible via manner of various human beings. Thinking that specific humans can see your insecurities will handiest make you sense privy to each motion, but now not displaying the ones insecurities builds up self guarantee.

Chapter 13: Discuss your emotions

It is always better to talk approximately your feelings in vicinity of keeping they all inner. If you can't find out a person whom you may talk your feelings with, a journal and/or a blog is an proper enough alternative.

Remember that you create your private destiny

Do no longer allow distinctive humans to control your existence—in mind, in phrases or in motion. You control your very personal existence, and your picks are your personal, now not others'.

Take risks to trade your behavior

It isn't always easy to remove your insecurities. In truth, it is a whole lot less complicated to stay with them in area of cast off them. Still, you need to think long-time period in phrases of vital alternatives for your life. Always preserve in thoughts the lengthy-term benefits and no longer the quick-time period ones because of the truth it is those in the long run that count the maximum.

Develop braveness inner yourself

Alongside taking dangers, you need to boom braveness inside your self due to the reality braveness is the maximum important special characteristic to very own if you want to preserve with something. Without braveness, you couldn't be capable of do something else. It all starts with the strength of mind to collect some issue.

Consider the poor outcomes of loss of confidence

Know that insecurity gets you nowhere. Remember what you are placing at hazard if making a decision to stay together together with your insecurities.

Think of the amazing effects of overcoming lack of self assurance

The amazing effects of overcoming lack of confidence can also feature your motivating pressure. Always preserve your mind outstanding and those will translate to movements.

Always be actual

In the whole thing you do, take into account to constantly live real. Stay right to yourself and to others that lets in you to make the manner of defeating your insecurities worthwhile and true.

Learn to permit bypass of the subjects that make you insecure

Do not pick out to hold at once to the subjects that make you insecure. It may be hard as some matters may be pricey to you, but something that stops you from making picks on your very very own isn't first rate for you; consequently, they should be set free.

Accept the subjects which you can't alternate

No bear in mind how an entire lot you need to alternate your life completely, there are some topics that you cannot alternate. Acceptance of this truth is one component, on the identical time as embracing the ones eternal matters is another.

Maintain a healthful life-style

Insecurity isn't limited to the mental and intellectual domain names of the body. In aiming to triumph over your biggest insecurities, you need to also be aware about the physical body. Remember that bodily health interprets to intellectual, emotional and intellectual fitness.

Work on putting off your insecurities one after the opportunity

Nothing may be done in handiest a single step. Instead of on the lookout for to take shortcuts, take one step at a time at the same time as eliminating your insecurities. This way, you can live more targeted for your assignment, and you may collect greater productiveness.

Develop your talents to reinforce your arrogance

Being decided to combat your insecurities is one manner of supporting your self, however you need to assist your self similarly and till the give up. You understand that low arrogance is one in each of the most crucial symptoms of lack of self notion, and at the way to solve the bigger trouble, start with coping with the smaller ones. Help yourself thru growing your abilities at the manner to raise your vanity.

Start taking motion

Lastly, in case you need for those tips to take effect, then you definitely definately need to begin via taking movement. None of those portions of recommendation will translate to fact till you do as such. Nonetheless, may additionally additionally the ones hints serve their purpose not surely in precept, but greater importantly, in workout.

Chapter 14: How To Overcome Them.

I anticipate the fastest manner to overcome insecurities is to #1 admit which you have them in the first region.

Then find out the feelings you would love to take their location.

Then end up aware of the moves you need to now take.

Your cutting-edge insecurities might also additionally additionally sense very scary but recognize that they'll be handiest short.

Don't be intimidated via your insecurities, you're the most effective who created them for your thoughts and YOU are the only who can do away with them with endurance, mild love and care and time.

You conquer your insecurities through having the braveness to stand them and to renowned what they're.

You overcome them with the aid of manner of talking lifestyles into the truth which you're a movie star.

You are the movie star of your global, now not your insecurities.

You make your insecurities take a backseat and deplete while making a decision that it's your insecurities you're going to defeat and upward push up for your very very very own ft.

You overcome your insecurities with the useful resource of way of taking your power back and faraway from them.

You decide that you're not going to be beneath their spell nor be controlled via them.

You triumph over your insecurities by the usage of talking Life into yourself.

Speaking pinnacle on yourself is right for your mental, spiritual, physical & emotional fitness.

Your insecurities had been speculated to shake you not ruin you.

You conquer your insecurities with the aid of not being shaken with the beneficial resource of them.

You get a keep of them.

You manage them in preference to letting them manage you.

Find out what your insecurities are approximately.

Write them down and allow your self to determine them out.

When you well known your insecurities, they may weaken and your feel of safety within your self will give a lift to.

Once you do this, you're to your manner then.

Acknowledge wherein your ache factors are and what you're inclined to do approximately them.

Acknowledge if you could do something about them.

And if you may, at the same time as are you able to begin on foot on those changes.

To enhance your insecurities, it's in fact about transferring your mentality.

Your insecurities are simplest a reflected photo of in which you are mentally.

How to procure there may be a remarkable story altogether and that's okay.

What's most crucial is which you take the right steps you want to make trade.

Body Weight

Body weight may be a very sensitive state of affairs matter in phrases of emotions of lack of confidence.

Some humans enjoy that their body is supposed to shield them, giving them a experience of safety.

When human beings enjoy betrayed with the aid in their frame, that is what creates a few lack of confidence.

When they don't enjoy like their frame is a real mirrored photograph of the way they need it to appearance, every now and then they will be and experience overtook.

Feeling overtook with the resource in their frame no longer cooperating with them.

Feeling like their frame weight doesn't serve them well and is some kind of sin.

Your body is meant in an effort to charge it at irrespective of what weight or length you're currently at.

This is right and real no matter in case you're thin, in among or fats.

Body weight is a few thing you may manage for the most element if you decide to art work at that.

You are in truth on top of things over your very own frame.

150

Becoming targeted and on pinnacle of things over your very private body must grow to be more than simply taken into consideration one of your preferred hobbies.

A lot of frame insecurities come from people comparing their non-public body to distinct human beings's.

What someone else has taking place with their frame has nothing to do with you.

Having a frame picture or weight problem need to imply which you need to be focusing extra on you.

Your frame is your frame and you've got the strength to mentally change some thing it's far you do no longer like approximately it.

Your body is your body and you need to embrace it.

If it's an loss of self assurance of yours, you need to face it.

Even extra than your frame, you're a Spirit.

Learn to Love the Spirit inner of you and collectively along side your body you becomes more comfortable.

Beyond your weight, your frame ought to generally be very vital to you.

Your frame is in which your organs are stored and gives your stunning Spirit a place to stay.

Your frame is in reality really worth you treasuring and you want to treat it that manner no matter how masses you weigh.

You have to nourish your our bodies with the good food and drinks it wishes in case you want to flourish.

More important than your body weight, the power that your body possesses is truely as precious.

Cherish and price your body, whether or now not you weigh one hundred twenty five or 192, it does not be counted variety due to the fact your body is part of you.

What Others Say Doesn't Matter.

One of the precept reasons you may revel in insecure is due to the truth you're retaining onto what someone or a few humans might also moreover have said approximately you.

Or probable you're involved approximately what others may furthermore or will say approximately you.

Either manner, you your self regardless of what changed into or may be said, must consider which you are exquisite.

You want to no longer allow what different humans have stated or can also say get to you.

It might be of no provider to you to internalize what they anticipate.

What specific humans recollect you need to now not be allowed the strength to make you lower.

What others have to mention approximately you need to now not contribute to any of your insecurities but sure we're all human and on occasion we're in a region in which we permit shit to get to us.

But you need to permit others anticipate what they assume due to the reality you and I both realise that there is lots more to us.

What others have to say approximately you or your Life is simply beside the factor.

Whether it become an ex-boyfriend, fling, friend, family member, decide, instructor, etc., it really doesn't count.

The tremendous opinion that surely topics is the only you have got of your self, so your opinion of your self ought to be appropriate in your fitness.

You type of want to permit others human beings's opinion of you roll off your again.

I understand that counting on in which you are, it's not continuously easy like that.

This is why you have to assemble this sort of robust bond with your self that nobody can damage it.

Your relationship with your self wants to be healed definitely so no person can break it.

Your relationship with yourself desires to be stable just so no person can rock it.

So that no man or woman can throw you off path or make you experience more insecure than you could already enjoy.

The opinion coming from your self is the simplest opinion that need to ever enjoy actual.

Never are seeking out others approval due to the fact undergo in thoughts what they have got to mention has not anything to do with you.

You CAN get decrease again on Top!

You may have fallen off in Life at one component like I certainly have however this isn't always a purpose to continuously revel in insecure or mad.

Trust Me I get it, at the same time as you fall off it brings a whole lot of fears to the ground for you, which includes: How am I going to live on? And What am I going to do?

Do understand that that is simplest brief boo.

You can absolutely get lower lower lower back on Top!!!

Little thru the usage of little you'll turn out to be assured enough which you gained't be able to be stopped.

So don't save you attempting, working on and enhancing yourself.

You can get decrease again on pinnacle absolutely.

You might also moreover have in no way belief you may fall off and might have even been in surprise.

But do understand which you have the capacity to go back decrease again lower decrease returned stronger than you ever have earlier than due to the reality you understand now and characteristic the machine to get yourself once more up off the ground.

You now have determined energy that you didn't even recognize you had.

Now you recognize you have got the functionality to deal with any greater problems in the event that they ever stumble upon your course.

Being on the Top of your interest isn't always out of reap for you, you simply need to understand that this is not what's going to create that stable protection inside you.

You can not depend upon "Success" to make you experience properly inner.

You need to experience pinnacle inner regardless as to what you own or in which you're dwelling.

But do Know which you CAN get over again on Top, a few element Top manner for you.

Maybe it way now not having any issues and letting your herbal electricity go together with the glide through you.

Maybe it way without a doubt doing a little element it is that you need to do.

Whatever which means that for you in reality recognize that it's now not out of your acquire, you just sense briefly caught due to your insecurities.

Chapter 15: Security Doesn't Have Contingencies.

Your revel in of protection must never have contingencies.

Obviously except to your primary survival goals.

Beyond that, you shouldn't want a big residence or severa cash to experience steady.

Do no longer limit on the identical time as you could get entry to all of your enjoy of safety that's in keep.

Do not restriction even as you'll be able to enjoy more.

Do no longer limit whilst and the way your protection can come approximately.

Your enjoy of protection need to in no way be based totally on outdoor effects.

That is the way you positioned your self up for catastrophe due to the fact if some factor is going wrong to your worldwide, your sense of safety may additionally additionally save you.

That is truly now not the manner you get decrease back on Top!

Your sense of protection need to additionally in no manner come from outsiders and what they think about you and your Life.

"If one-of-a-kind human beings suppose I definitely have this and that then i'll be stable in others eyes." NO!!!

That is Not how this works.

Your feel of protection moreover shouldn't ever come out of your fame or administrative center.

Your revel in of protection want to come from the soil, like on this earth.

Your experience of safety need to surely come from expertise your nicely worth.

Your experience of safety want to in no way be tied to people, places and matters, it need to normally in reality be tied to and connected to what's internal.

What's interior is your Soul that knows…

Knows who you are and is not wanting anybody nor something to verify that.

Your feel of safety is impartial from some component that you can ever non-public, very very personal that.

Your experience of protection want to no longer come from whether or not or now not or now not people together with you or need to be with you.

Never tie your protection to what someone nor woman sees in you.

In order to truly turn out to be sturdy, you have to allow skip of the humans pleaser in you.

Your safety does now not come from how well you may please and what you could do.

Your protection constantly, want to return from You.

Qualities Of Secure People.

Secure people have the capability to look and enjoy bs without letting it overtake them.

Secure human beings have the capability to permit criticism or even a few compliments roll off their lower once more.

They have the capability to interest on what it's far they have got in preference to what it's far they lack.

Secure human beings have the capability to peer past others evaluations of themselves.

Secure human beings regularly don't criticize themselves.

Secure human beings recognize whilst topics, people and places are wholesome for them and at the identical time as they will be no longer.

Secure humans apprehend sincerely who they may be even in the crowd of hundreds and thousands of human beings.

Secure people write their own Life memories, create their private movies and the sequels.

Secure people don't see people above them but as their equal.

Secure human beings have the capability to keep to realise their well in reality really worth regardless of how normally they've been harm.

Secure people have the potential to recognize that in which others think they may be of their lives doesn't count number wide variety.

Secure humans recognize that how they experience about in which they'll be in their private lives is all that topics.

Secure humans permit people speak shit with out it negatively effecting them.

Secure people don't permit specific humans's terrible opinions of them to be stressing them.

Secure people don't allow what others have to mention approximately them sink into their hearts and Spirits.

Secure human beings are not afraid to percent with the arena, the methods wherein they're proficient and gifted.

Secure people recognise that feeling insecure is most effective short for them.

They apprehend how other people may additionally moreover additionally experience about them doesn't sincerely scare them.

They understand and understand that people are entitled to their non-public opinion however they do no longer should pay interest.

Secure humans recognize how to maneuver through awful energies and vibes and discover their tribes.

Secure humans recognize that their happiness comes first.

Secure human beings recognize that no one honestly has the electricity to guide them to experience like dirt.

Secure human beings have the power to decipher among what's actual and what's now not.

Secure people recognize that they're it and they're heat.

Secure human beings understand that they've what it takes to ascend to the pinnacle.

Secure humans understand who they certainly are and who they're not.

Secure human beings don't experience like they ought to attempt to continuously show a factor.

Secure people realize they have got the capacity to be and experience on factor.

Secure people don't are looking for validation from others.

Secure human beings have the functionality to continuously be their true self, no want to position on mask or covers.

eight.Don't Be Afraid You Feel That Way.

Don't be afraid that you could presently experience insecure, it happens, we're human.

Don't be afraid that you're doomed and going to revel in this manner all the time, that is not actual.

By you reading this e-book it's far clean and obvious which you want higher for you.

Pain and ache is most effective quick.

When you intentionally determine which you want to experience robust internal yourself, by using nature this is the course that you may skip in.

By nature this is the energy on the way to start flowing.

In the period in-between in among time, don't be afraid that you are feeling insecure now and again.

The quicker you may admit it, the quicker you could take away it.

Don't be afraid that your insecurities are going to drown you out, however the reality that you may experience like they will had been doing that for some time now.

Don't be afraid that your insecurities are going to torture you currently because of the truth you've got got the power to alternate them now.

You have the energy to exchange the way you remember in that you are and in which you've been.

You have the energy to sincerely & deeply float internal.

You have the energy to understand in addition to famend what's occurring internal of you.

You have the electricity to determine that you're prepared to grow inner you.

You have the electricity to hobby in a way that lets in your insecurities to decrease inside you.

No One Is Judging You That Harshly.

You may additionally additionally currently feel clowned or made amusing of, like simply every person can see or fragrance your insecurities but absolutely understand and understand that no one is certainly judging you that harshly.

No one is absolutely seeing all of these insecurities that you see & enjoy.

Recognize that it's miles YOU who is the usage of your self loopy with all of these insecurities to your thoughts, you need to prevent thinking those insecure mind so your experience of safety can heal.

Stop over exaggerating and blowing up your insecurities, they'll be no longer as massive as you're making them out to be.

Sure you could use some upgrades in sure areas, but calm your self down, loosen up and permit your self be.

Again, no individual is judging you that harshly.

Fall in Love with enjoyable your body and overcoming your insecurities due to the fact your insecurities are inflicting you to panic and create a fake reality.

Your faux fact of insecurities isn't always serving you nicely.

Do yourself a choose and permit your self to excel.

Do your self a pick and permit your coronary heart, mind, frame and Soul to move out of that insecure place.

Allow yourself to actually decorate your intellectual and emotional state.

Do yourself a choice and permit yourself to allow pass.

What if your insecurities are not real?

What in case you are misinterpreting the manner you surely experience?

What if you can located yourself in a completely precise state of mind at the same time as you unwind?

What if you can launch every lack of self assurance you have were given with a easy bubble bathtub?

What if all your insecurities are made up to your head?

What if you have psyched your self out into believing you are useless?

What if there definitely is not any purpose in an effort to experience down approximately your self?

What if all of your insecurities are truely lies you tell yourself?

What if no individual may even visibly see any of your insecurities?

What in case you're freaking out over not anything?

What if you're creating a small minor element that you may easily tweak and fix proper proper right into a big massive some thing?

What if you'll revel in better about yourself in case you honestly calmed down a chunk?

What if who you're and in which you are right now could be proper?

What if who you are right now will be exactly sufficient???

What if you're extra than enough?

What if you created a large nightmare to your head for no motive?

What in case you are stressing your heart and frame out for no cause?

What if now might be clearly your season?

What in case your insecurities disappeared through you believing?

Chapter 16: Listen To Your Affirmations.

When you're going thru a totally insecure time to your Life, it is truely important to pay attention to your affirmations.

I'd noticeably advise taking note of Rockstar Affirmations on YouTube, that channel is truely going that will help you reprogram your thoughts for Success and help produce terrific feelings of protection.

Affirmations have the strength to take you from where you're to wherein you'd need to be.

I cannot particular enough how an entire lot being attentive to Affirmations have helped Me.

Affirmations have helped Me plenty on My direction to becoming mentally, emotionally, spiritually and bodily free.

Affirmations have helped Me to carve out a higher Me.

Listen to your affirmations, they may be free.

173

They will allow you to come to be the whole thing you honestly want to be, believe Me.

Your Affirmations may be in a feature that will help you forged out all negativity.

They will assist you to truely see your capability and the strength of your highbrow.

Listening to affirmations can take you from feeling insecure to feeling like you can triumph over the area.

Of path relying on in which you're, this won't virtually display up in a unmarried day.

You must positioned them on repeat and concentrate to them every day, day and night time time time.

Affirmations, at the same time as you trust in them, have the strength to take you to new heights.

They will have you seeing new elements of hobby.

Please do accept as proper with in the hype.

Affirmations have helped Me with topics collectively with: heartbreaks, anxiety, depression and absence of self belief.

Give it a hazard and allow it to do the identical for you and will assist you to create internal safety.

Affirmations on my own may not in reality do the venture but they positive as hell can help you open up your mind.

Affirmations let you to pick out your head up and recall who you're.

They permit you to to enjoy higher about your self and boom your emotions of feeling as lots as par.

Affirmations will will let you to manipulate your insecure emotions generating thoughts.

They can help you get your thoughts underneath control.

They help empower you and allow you to look which you truely have the power and are in control.

You Have Time, Relax.

A lot of the time our insecurities come from feeling like we don't have sufficient time.

Like we don't have sufficient time to get ourselves together or to do this element that we actually need to do.

But I am right right here to inform you that you really do.

You certainly do have the time which you're seeking out.

You simply do have the time to do all that you choice and extra.

What is the push?

Are you dashing to reveal a aspect? Or to look proper in others eyes?

Are you speeding because of the truth you feel such as you don't have sufficient time to be alive?

Are you speeding due to the reality you revel in like you have to have and be doing greater to your Life?

Whatever areas of your Life which you're insecure about, recognize that you may typically decorate in them, regardless of what instances they arrive approximately.

You don't ought to do everything proper away and don't sense the want to faux like you have got were given it altogether.

You don't want to deliver an purpose of to each person in which you're for your Life.

Life isn't a race and you can pass at your very very own pace.

Get it from your mind which you should be doing some thing else in this place and time...

Because I can assure which you are precisely wherein you want to be to take the following main steps of your Life.

Feel confident and deliver your self a hazard to get it proper.

Relax and stay calm.

Don't become cold with yourself, stay warmness.

And no, time is not walking out.

There isn't any buzzer or timer you need to beat.

Have staying energy with yourself and apprehend that things will turn out neat.

Everything to your Life is unfolding because it need to.

They may be hard as a manner to understand inside the within the meantime but try it if you can.

Know that component is in your aspect.

You do no longer ever want to try to beat time.

And moreover understand from the depths of your being that point is an phantasm in this vicinity and time.

Relax and breathe, Life isn't always a opposition without a doubt.

Don't stress yourself out looking to play entice up with a person else's Life.

Trust your self and your machine and you'll be ok.

1So What!

One of the most crucial keys to liberating your insecurities is to not make a large deal out of factors.

So what if you nonetheless stay at your mother's house!

So what in case you didn't get that excessive paying gadget but!

So what if you aren't precisely in that you want to be but!

Live your Life with no regrets.

You are not right proper here on the planet to reveal any factors to all people.

You don't owe every body an proof.

You don't owe all of us a conversation.

You are in that you're and that's good enough!

As extended as you're running on transferring ahead your way!

You want to Live a pressure free existence?? Then take it smooth.

You aren't proper right here to make your Life hard however to make it breezy.

So what if you don't have a automobile genuinely however!

So what in case you don't have a house genuinely however!!!

So what! So what! So what!

Stop developing a big deal out of factors.

Yeah probably your ego is a bit harm and bruised, this may be actual.

But that does not advise that need to cast off from your capability to clearly be you.

Everybody's ego receives banged up and bruised up every so often.

Stop growing a large deal out of factors and decide now.

Decide now which you're going to allow yourself to be free and not positioned all of those suggestions and rules on your being.

No there may be no such rule that announces you want to be at a positive location or have a certain amount of things with the resource of a particular age.

There is not the form of element like that.

By whose e-book do you make a decision to play?

Whose requirements are you searching for to stay as much as besides?

Who on this planet are you searching for to please?

Relax and fill your thoughts pretty genuinely, do no longer buy into the idea that you are proper proper here to delight.

Do no longer buy into the concept that your dreams are your wishes.

Do no longer buy into the concept that you want to be eager to satisfaction.

Do now not be as lots as no first-rate and inclusive of up a few more insecurities.

Do now not be up to no accurate and emerge as your very own enemy.

Truly get to comprehend, line up and sync up with the man or woman you name "Me".

Focus to your holiday spot not in which you currently are.

No depend what your current-day state of affairs you need to feel like a celeb.

You are the Star of your worldwide.

The mild of your Life.

You have the power to permit move of all of your insecurities all day and night time time time. thirteen. Appreciate What You Do Have.

If your real cause is to begin to feel solid, you in fact want to begin focusing on and appreciating what you do have...

Because what you have got had been given is essential too.

Don't be someone who overlooks the advantages which have already been brought to you.

Don't be a pessimist who's always complaining about shit, be a person who grabs life by means of the usage of manner of the balls, and well-knownshows the high-quality matters in all of it.

Appreciate the presence of the notable matters for your Life.

Appreciate the presence of all the topics on your Life which are proper.

Appreciate the health that you do have, ensure you revel in robust about that.

Your unique health is a real luxury and a few human beings don't have that.

Appreciate the presence of your right working limbs.

Appreciate the presence of all that's appropriate internal.

Appreciate the presence of your cutting-edge progressions.

Appreciate the statistics you've acquired and all the training.

Appreciate the presence of your sanity, bear in mind Me a few people honestly don't have this. Lol

Appreciate the mind that you do have.

Appreciate the electricity that you do have.

Appreciate the little little little bit of protection which you possibly do have and assemble on that.